Done

and

Been

Done

Steel Rail Chronicles

and

of American Hobos

Been

Gypsy Moon

A National Queen of the Hobos

Indiana University Press BLOOMINGTON & INDIANAPOLIS

The paper used in this publication meets the minimum requirements of
American National Standard for Information Sciences—Permanence of
Paper for Printed Library Materials, ANSI Z39.48-1984.

MANUFACTURED IN THE UNITED STATES OF AMERICA

Library of Congress Cataloging-in-Publication Data

Gypsy Moon.
    Done and been : steel rail chronicles of American hobos / Gypsy Moon.
      p.   cm.
    Includes bibliographical references.
    ISBN 0-253-32985-X (cl : alk. paper). — ISBN 0-253-21035-6 (pa : alk.
paper)
    1. Tramps—United States—History. 2. Tramps—United States—
Interviews. I. Title.
HV4505.G93   1996
305.5'68—dc20   95-18796

1   2   3   4   5   01   00   99   98   97   96

Dedicated to
my father and mother for the lessons,
my family for the love and patience,
my professors Robert Kirch and Ed Casebeer for the encouragement,
and my brothers and sisters in the wind.

Contents

A Hobo's Daughter

Gentle Memories

I recall my father tucking me into bed at night. His large hands, in a single brusque gesture, would flip up the left edge of the mattress, then allow it to snap back again magically against the box springs, capturing the entire length of the bedcovers in its grip. As this feat was repeated on the right, the familiar tightness of the blankets pressed against my childish frame, cocooning me under the sheets. When he sat down next to me, his weight on the already tautly stretched covers would double their unyielding hold, forcing me to turn slightly toward him. The view of my father from this angle was as familiar to me as the hobo stories and songs that he presented in each of these nocturnal performances.

Much of the beauty of my childhood was born out of my father's honesty. He dared to be himself, allowing me to see his weaknesses as well as his strengths. He shared with me, through his talents as a singer and storyteller, not only the settled years after he met my mother but also the precarious, footloose years of his youth. I would gaze up at him from my pillow, waiting for him to spin another colorful saga, and from this cozy vantage point beneath my covers, I would again become his most receptive audience.

He called these moments "Jackie's time." While other children were hearing Mother Goose, I thrilled to adventures of my dad's real-life experiences. The stories were varied accounts of his hoboing days—riding the rods, jumping a rattler, or camping in the jungles—after he left his home in 1911 at the age of thirteen. I might hear about running moonshine or dodging revenuers in the Blue Ridge Mountains near his childhood home of Frog Level, North Carolina. Perhaps he would paint a graphic verbal picture for me of the West Coast opium dens, or relive dance marathons, shotgun weddings, and short-lived jail terms. While the topic was unpredictable, I could always count on the story being followed by a song.

The rule was that I could choose one each night from his repertoire, which he had committed to memory during his years around the campfires of hobo jungles. I would choose from such titles as "My Consumptious Sarah Jane," "Get You a Kitchen Mechanic from the White Folks' Yard," "Hallelujah, I'm a Bum," or my favorite, "Cocaine Jubilee." He had a deep southern voice, which he accompanied on the guitar. He would pick up his worn instrument and begin to strum:

> Down at that Cocaine Jubilee,
> Down on the isles of H., M., and C.
> H. is for heroine, M. is for morph,
> C. is for cocaine. It can blow your noodle off.

> We'll buy a hundred hypos, all wrapped in pearls,
> And every old dope fiend will bring along his girl,
> Every fellow with a habit, jumping like a rabbit,
> Down at that Cocaine Jubilee.

> Way down yonder in New Orleans,
> Baby's in the cradle sniffing good ole cocaine.
> Go away doctor, don't you change her mind.
> She wants another sniff of that good old crystalline.

> Well, coke was made for horses and not for dirty men.
> The doctor says it'll kill you, but he didn't say when!

> If there ain't no cocaine up in heaven,
> I don't want to go there.
> I don't want to ride no golden chariot
> Or sit in a golden chair.

> Oh! Sniffing good ole cocaine—boys, that's my pride.
> Me and St. Peter's gonna take a hayride!

Sometimes he would throw in an extra—a song of his choice, which was usually a rambling song. These were his favorites, and for years I believed that those reckless themes with the carefree melodies had been written about him.

And so it is little wonder that my heart has been in tune over the years with life's free spirits.

Done

and

Been

1.

A Short Course in Hoe Boy History and Philosophy

My curiosity, having been piqued by my father's hobo songs and stories, led me to begin research on the topic at Indiana University (Indianapolis) better than ten years ago. When I needed a topic for an independent writing course, the decision was an easy one. I wanted to learn more about the era that had been so much a part of my father's life.

After discovering that the hobos still hold a convention in Britt, Iowa, I contacted that town's chamber of commerce, and the people there put me in touch with a few of the oldtimers. Encouraged by the possibility of talking with folks who had actually lived the lifestyle during its heyday, I decided to use an oral history approach to the topic. Our state archivist gave me an afternoon crash course on how to conduct the interviews, and with my tape recorder and my steno pad in hand, I set off in search of subjects.

My first contact was with Steamtrain Maury, who had spent two major segments of his life on the road—once for several years as a young man, and again throughout his fifties, leaving a wife and two nearly grown daughters behind. The chamber suggested that I interview him first, since he had long been considered the hobos' elder statesman and goodwill ambassador. That initial interview was made by phone. I explained that I was working on a college research project and proceeded down my carefully compiled list of questions. He responded like a man who had been interviewed many times. At first his answers seemed too smooth, too rote. But then later, after I mentioned that my father had been a hobo for many years, there was an unexpected shift. He began to ask *me* questions! Suddenly, without ever having seen one another, without knowing more than five minutes of background about each other, there was a bond. "You must come to the convention in Britt," he urged. "That little town has been the home of the national convention since the year 1900!" I promised to consider his invitation.

When August came around, I felt that my calendar was too full to attend, but at the last moment a window opened. I called airlines. The closest a commercial flight would land was Des Moines, better than a two-hour drive to Britt. I continued making calls. No train service to Britt. No bus service. I eventually decided to fly to Des Moines, rent a car, and drive the two hours from the airport. Then I wondered if it would be possible to get a hotel or motel room on such short notice. I called the chamber of commerce. The director chuckled politely, "This is Britt, Iowa, Jackie. We don't have any hotels . . . and the only little motel out on the highway has been booked up for months."

"That's no problem," I responded, "I can just stay at a nearby campground."

There was a pause. "Well, there is a little campground, but it's sure not nearby," she added. "Hold on a second. I see Steamtrain walking up the street."

I heard the receiver hit the countertop, then a moment later Steamtrain's familiar voice was giving me instructions. "Honey, you just bring along an old bedroll and stay right out in the jungle with the rest of us."

Envisioning myself sleeping amid a crowd of men straight off the iron road, I asked tactfully, "Do you think I'll feel comfortable doing that?"

"Comfortable?" He sounded puzzled. "Ain't you never slept out on the ground before? Why, we'll just put down a couple pieces of cardboard under your roll, and you'll sleep like a baby!"

I was glad he couldn't see me smiling. "Oh, no, Steamtrain," I explained more directly. "I'm a camper and okay with all that. I'm just wondering about a woman staying in a jungle of men."

The light bulb turned on in his voice. "Oooh," he said understandingly, "you don't have to worry about that at all. You won't be the only woman. Why, old Slo Freight Ben's already here."

"Well, by golly," I thought determinedly, "if old Slo Freight can do it, so can I!"

Two days later I arrived at my first hobo jungle along the Soo Rail Line in Britt. I identified myself to Steamtrain and spent the next few days feeling like the Lord had miraculously given me a week with my father twenty times over. When I left Britt that Sunday morning, my duffle bag was loaded with tapes, notebooks, and rolls of film, recording a week of stories, music, and images. My life would never be the same again.

In the months following my trip to Britt, I focused primarily on the few oldtimers who were still living. I was particularly interested in taping stories of the handful who were still on the road. Many of the older men I interviewed reminded me in various ways of my father, and close friendships began to flourish.

As more and more hobos became my friends, I became more and more a part of their community. Soon I was being assigned various tasks, such as helping to establish a memorial cemetery where hobos can be buried alongside their brothers, and raising money to support a hobo museum. Both are in Britt, Iowa, and are managed by the National Hobo Foundation, a not-for-profit organization that is committed to preserving hobo history. Later I became a member of that foundation, and during the 1990 hobo convention, I was elected a National Queen of the Hobos.

The hobos whom I interviewed were, in the beginning, simply a source of primary research; today, they are a fundamental support system in my life, and I feel accepted fully into their community. I consider many of them family.

Because this vast network of friends is geographically scattered across the country or living on the road as they move from job to job, we rely on letters and phone calls as means of sustaining our community. Throughout the year, I travel to various locations to jungle up with groups of them in small towns, beside the railroad tracks, or along river banks and to enjoy the strong fraternity that has been characteristic of this subculture for more than a century.

History

Through my research and my friendships in this community, I have developed an understanding and respect for the culture and lifestyle that has set this group of vagabonds apart from their ne'er-do-well counterparts.

The American hobo was a free-spirited adventurer, crusty, resourceful, and adaptable—a hardworking, proud, yet often alienated dreamer. "He was homeless . . . freeloaded on the freight trains whose tracks he laid and whose tunnels he blasted. . . . He was a unique and indigenous American product" (Allsop x). With his bindle of belongings on his back, he wandered the continent— transported by the rails he laid, through the fields and groves he harvested, the prairies he fenced, the forests he cleared, past the mines, oil fields, and canals his labor had helped create. He was "a reckless, perambulating soldier of fortune" ("Hobo"). His journey was as uncertain as the elements he weathered and his personality as rich as the scattered legacy he left behind.

The chronicle of the American hobo is connected inextricably to the railroads. By the end of the Civil War, a scant 30,000 miles of iron veined its way across the continent, the embryonic form of a new lifeblood. The advent of the railroad vitalized the nation's economy by highballing a wealth of goods and raw materials to ports and factories. The expanding network was already cutting deeply into the vastness and character of the West as it wooed—with a persistent and romantic call—a second wave of frontiersmen. The whistle of the steam engine called millions to work on rails thrusting persistently west. Among the workers were thousands of Civil War veterans, reluctant or unable after the experience of war to settle down. Each new spike drove the able-bodied laborers farther from home and family as the girders continued to advance. The 1880s added 70,000 miles of new track, and railroad jobs were in abundance for those who desired the work. However, when the nation's economy faltered, leading to the deflationary spiral of the 1890s, millions were left jobless. Some returned home in the wake of the 1894 depression; many did not.

The search for work and a restless disposition kept many of them moving. And the rails they had laid, eventually stretching 254,000 miles, became their means of mobility. Thus emerged the American hobo.

The origin of the term *hobo* is uncertain, but a number of explanations are offered. Godfrey Irwin, in *American Tramp and Underworld Slang*, proposes that it could be a derivative "from the Latin *homo bonus*, or *good man;* others say that the word was first used after the Civil War in the United States, where soldiers walking home through the country replied, *Homeward bound*, when questioned as to their destination. . . . [Others] assert that the strolling musicians who played on the hautboy [oboe] were the first hoboes" (100). The more accepted notion is that it is the description of a young man seeking garden work, "a hoe boy." Whatever the term's source, the word *hobo*, according to Allsop, was in general use in the last half of the nineteenth century (104).

Although there is still some disagreement among hobos and historians, the sociologist Nels Anderson presents a well-accepted definition of this new breed in his 1923 book, *The Hobo*. It distinguishes hobos from other vagabonds. Assessing previous studies, Anderson concluded that the hobo was a migratory worker, a person traveling in search of employment with seasonal crops, in mills, shops, or mines, or at other jobs that might become available. Hobos today—young and old alike—adamantly agree. "There's one thing I'd like people to get into their mind," argues Alabama Hobo, like a preacher in his pulpit. "A hobo is a drifting worker. A worker. Follows his trade, and if he can't get a job at his trade, he does other work. But a bum, he's just a bum!"

The tramp, by comparison, was a migratory nonworker with a passion for seeing the country without earning his way. He was "a specialist at 'getting by,' . . . an easy-going individual who lives from hand to mouth for the mere joy of living" (Anderson 94). He frequently requested door-to-door handouts and accepted mission help. However, many oldtimers like Steamtrain Maury Graham contend that tramps were simply "men that walked wherever they went. The word *tramp* means walker; it's that simple, walker."

Finally, Anderson defines the more stationary *bum* and *homeguard*. The bum was a ne'er-do-well nonworker, who lived in one place and usually indulged excessively in liquor or drugs. Consequently, the bum also depended on handouts and mission assistance. The term *homeguard* refers to the unskilled day laborer who stayed in one town but lived on the main stem (skid row), the area of the town most frequented by those down-and-outs (96). Hobos often quote the 1930s physician Dr. Ben L. Reitman, who once lived on the road: "The hobo works and wanders, the tramp dreams and wanders and the bum drinks and wanders" (Anderson 87).

While there are differing definitions and opinions, all seem to agree on one point: Hobos were committed to the work ethic. Though they experienced the pangs of hardship that labor shortages bring, they opted to work rather than panhandle.

From the outset, hobos experienced solidarity, sharing philosophies, hardships, and resources. In 1894, history saw the first public, organized effort involving hobos. "General" Jacob S. Coxey, an Ohio businessman, marched on Washington with a motley "army" of about five hundred jobless demonstrators. They were requesting a public works project that would provide jobs for the unemployed, but when they finally arrived at the nation's Capitol, they were dispersed by club-carrying policemen. These callous actions convinced many Americans that the Cleveland administration had little concern for those struggling through an economic depression (Garraty 614), and the jobless—among them migratory hobos—had strengthened their fraternity.

Over the years, migrants expressed themselves through other efforts that grew from this unrest. Anderson writes: "Among the organizations initiated or promoted by migrants are the Industrial Workers of the World (I.W.W.), the International Brotherhood of Welfare Association (I.B.W.A.), the Migratory Workers Union (M.W.U.), and United Brotherhood of American Laborers" (230).

THE HARVEST STIFF'S "TIPPERARY"

You've paid the going wages, that's kept us on the bum.
You say you've done your duty, you chin-whiskered-son-
　　of-a-gun.
But now long wintery breezes are a shaking our poor
　　frames,
And the long drawn days of hunger try to drive us boys
　　insane.
It is driving us to action; we are organized today.
Us pesky tramps and hobos are coming back to stay.

—Pat Brennen, IWW Protest Songwriter (Milburn 104)

The Industrial Workers of the World emerged in 1905. Monotony, long hours, and low pay had long been problems for the job-seeking hobo. Previously, unions had provided leadership only to workers sharing a common trade. The IWW, on the other hand, attempted—at least theoretically—to unite all industrial workers, yet the hobo in particular has always been associated with it. With biting propaganda, intimidation, and fire-and-brimstone stump speakers, the Wobblies, as the organization became known, grew in membership and radical philosophy. In retrospect it is difficult to determine how many hobos bought IWW Red Cards as supporters and how many purchased them merely for protection. Wobbly recruiters, armed with pick handles and flaming rhetoric, checked the cards of hobos as they rode trains during harvest seasons. Many oldtime 'bos claim to have carried the cards simply to avoid beatings by Wobbly organizers.

The organization's commitment to abolish America's wage system struck fear into the hearts of government and business. President Wilson, Attorney General Mitchell Palmer, and the new Bureau of Investigation targeted the IWW during the Red Scare following World War I. Roger Bruns, in his book *Knights of the Road,* estimated, according to the IWW General Defense Committee, "that at the beginning of 1920 more than 2,000 Wobs were in jail for sedition, disloyalty, criminal syndicalism, and vagrancy" (159). Internal conflict regarding IWW policy, coupled with government suppression, sapped the Wobblies' strength, sending them on the road to extinction.

The International Brotherhood of Welfare Association started in 1905 as well. Like the IWW it aimed at improving the life of the homeless and migratory worker, but it focused on "welfare work, brotherhood, and co-operation among the hobos" (Anderson 236) rather than political action. The IBWA was the brainchild of James Eads How, a man who left his wealthy family, wandered the country for a time with hobos and tramps, and eventually spent much of his fortune trying to improve their conditions. The organization was well known for establishing the Hobo Colleges that were set up in the main stems, or skid row areas, of cities. These colleges were actually forums for speakers and public discussion. Most operated only in the winter because the "students" went on the road in search of work during the remainder of the year (Anderson 237).

The Wobblies had lost popularity, and many felt a need for a new organization to address the concerns of the migratory worker. Consequently, in 1918 the IBWA formed the Migratory Workers Union. The MWU became most active in Indiana and Ohio but remained weak and ineffective throughout its short existence (Anderson 241).

Jeff Davis, still remembered as the "all-time King of the Hobos," began a fraternal order in 1908 called the Hoboes of America. Social activities, such as an annual hobo convention, were enjoyed by thousands. These conventions continue to be held every year in August at Britt, Iowa. A publication, the *Hobo News,* provided a means of expression for the more creative vagabonds who submitted songs, poems, and stories for distribution to readers. The May 17, 1937, issue of *Time* describes the *Hobo News:*

> The journal . . . is like no other paper on earth. It is a peach and saffron tabloid full of hand-me-down line drawings and photographs of celebrated sun-downers, sentimental verse, advertisements of rabbits' feet and "surprise novelties," personalities and good advice. Founded last year as a quarterly, the *Hobo News* was soon converted to a monthly. It is distributed in Manhattan by its editors, elsewhere by itinerants at 5 cents a copy—10 cents "if we can get it." ("For Hoboes")

Although such organizations stirred the hobos to share a more common identity, nowhere did they share their lives more fully with their brothers than in the jungles. "The jungle was our home," recalls Steamtrain Maury. These hobo camping spots sprang up across the country near railroad water tanks where trains often make brief stops, close to bridges that offered shelter from rain and wind, and—if possible—along lakes or rivers for fishing, cooking, bathing, or laundering. Only in a few instances, such as severe weather, were downtown flophouses preferred to the jungles.

The strict code of the jungles was familiar to all 'bos. All did their part, and the camp and its utensils were invariably left clean and ready for use by the next group that passed through. Fry Pan Jack, a hobo for "better than fifty-three years," recalls replacing what he used:

> Well, if you used it, your job was to go uptown and try to replace it. When you left, you left the next man something. You left him wood, you left him matches. You tried your best to leave him something.

However, the jungles did not exclusively shelter men. A 1932 article in the *Literary Digest* describes a different type of hobo:

Along this highway in the gathering gloom of the desert night, plodded a woman, hesitantly approaching the camp-fire. A hush settled over the surprised group of men as the features of the woman became more distinguishable in the glow of the fire.

She was a woman of sixty, at least. In her face was the strained expression of suffering. Alkali dust had settled upon her little felt hat and heavy black coat. The run-over, tattered shoes spoke plainly of the distance she had walked. Those men could not help but think of those hundreds of hot, weary desert miles she had been compelled to cross.

There was coffee for her. There always is coffee in the jungles. ("Ladies")

Women were not uncommon among the 'bos. In August of 1933 the *Nation* shocked readers with the results of a study by the Women's Bureau in Washington. Various social agencies cooperated in the survey of nearly eight hundred cities across the country and found 9,769 women moving from place to place unattached and homeless. The Women's Bureau estimated that the number probably represented only a fifth or sixth of the actual total ("Tramps").

The article raised a question: "Is the woman hobo a new manifestation of feminine rights or an evidence of old human wrongs?" Yet even while the reasons behind her emergence were being questioned, a February 1934 report by Walter Reckless in the *American Mercury* concluded, "Women are making pretty good hoboes as hoboes go" (175).

Hobo Reefer Charlie remembered many women. One "was a registered nurse. She always carried a clean uniform in her pack and nurse's shoes. . . . She'd get her clean uniform out, and her shoes, and comb her hair, fix it all up, and go right up on that floor and start treating patients."

For the hobos—both men and women—the jungle was a refuge, a harbor, a place of rest. There they were among their own kind, exchanging stories, singing songs, and sharing meals. There they learned which railroad yards to avoid, where jobs were available, and which train schedules had changed. Sick hobos were cared for there by other hobos. "Maybe two or three days' rest and a few little home remedies," Alabama Hobo remembers, "might get you perked up well enough to travel on." It was around the jungle campfire that they engaged in fellowship and established friendships that frequently lasted a lifetime.

If the jungle was a place of security for the hobo, life on the road was, by contrast, dangerous and hostile. The Pennsylvania Railroad police reported that between 1899 and 1902, on the Pennsylvania Railroad alone, two thousand train jumpers died and five hundred suffered injuries resulting in amputations (Bruns 46). Jumping trains required skill and agility. If the freight was boarded at a standstill, there was a risk of being found when the railroad police inspected; consequently, most climbed on as the train began to pull away and jumped off before it stopped in the yard. Such feats were difficult enough for the young and healthy and could be deadly for those older and slower. Each hobo had a way of judging what was safe. Alabama Hobo explained his safety strategy:

> You get in the stirrup, the very bottom step on the ladder, and when you see a clear place, you let your foot down and let it touch the ground firmly. If that foot flies up and hits you in the rump, that train is going too fast for you to get off.

The hobo was often met with hostility both on the road and in town. While some communities were more tolerant than others, he was rarely a welcome sight unless his labor was needed to bring in crops or to pick fruit. And when the harvest ended, so did his welcome. Municipal police continually herded hobos toward the rail and out of town, and the railroad police persistently herded them out of the boxcars and back into town. Joe Hill, an IWW songwriter who was executed in Utah in 1915, captured a public attitude that was all too familiar to the hobo:

(to the tune of "Tramp, Tramp, Tramp, the Boys Are Marching")

Tramp, tramp, tramp, keep on a-tramping.
Nothing doing here for you.
If I catch you 'round again,
You will wear the ball and chain.
Keep on a-tramping,
That's the best thing you can do. (Milburn 118)

While ordinary citizens over the years continued to look on with disapproval, they were perhaps slightly envious. After all, the hobos' style, though somewhat disturbing, boldly expressed the rugged qualities that were slowly slipping away from society.

While the number of remaining oldtimers is dwindling, I have gained an appreciation for the younger hobos. Though the road has changed, these new-generation 'bos—who may sport state-of-the-art backpacks with internal frames and tote railroad scanners—are carrying on an age-old tradition of earning a living on the move. Some hitchhike, some travel in old cars, and many still jump freights.

My study of hobo history, coupled with the friendships I had formed within the community, motivated me to focus on education. I had become the executive director of the Indiana Transportation Museum near Indianapolis. The museum's first annual Hobo Days Weekend was a tremendous crowd pleaser. Hobos shared stories with large groups of museum visitors. People are surprised to learn that in contrast to bums, hobos earned their way, making a significant contribution to America's early labor history. I have continued over the years to work with civic and community groups, radio and TV stations, newspapers, magazines, and classes of schoolchildren in an effort to educate the public about this misunderstood slice of American history.

Changes

While I set out to change the minds of others about hobos and their lifestyle, I was gradually making changes in my own life and philosophy as well. One major turn was a move from the city to the country.

While the decision to move to a tiny, isolated 1920s log cabin near a quiet village in southern Indiana was a difficult one, I have come to believe that there are times in life when we innately know what is best for us. Such revelations are gifts, and perhaps divine. Time and again, I have examined the complexity of this shift in my life, but—simply put—the choice was a deeply personal attempt to gain the peace and harmony that comes from living life consistent with one's beliefs.

I have been attracted to this region near Nashville, Indiana, for twenty years because of its eclectic composition. The hollers are dotted with second-, third-, and fourth-generation hill folk. In addition, these hills enjoy a stimulating artist colony dating back to the 1880s, when the renowned impressionist T. C. Steele moved here, attracted by the uncommon blue haze that often settles in the valleys. Other artists followed. The popularity of Brown County State Park and the charming village of Nashville attract thousands of tourists annually and draw many who move here after retirement. Adding to the local color are a couple of sizable communes which have survived since the hippie era of the 1960s. Life here is generally lived slowly and simply. I once heard a frustrated visitor from Indianapolis—a flatlander, as some locals call them—fume that "everything here operates on Brown County time." I smiled. Most in this area seem to prefer it that way.

It's easy to maintain privacy in the densely wooded terrain. While it is a remarkably peaceful community in both attitude and natural beauty, it is also rich in legend and lore. Though my mailing address is Nashville, I'm actually wedged in among remote little hamlets with whimsical names like Gnaw Bone, Bean Blossom, Booger Holler, and Needmore.

This departure from the mainstream has changed me. While I am far from contemplative, I translate the word *meditation* differently now than I did four years ago. For me it is no longer a state of mind achieved by sitting cross-legged for long, profound intervals, but a near-constant disposition of awareness and accord. I am usually alone here; yet I am seldom lonely, and I have come to accept my occasional periods of loneliness as comfortable challenges.

Such a lifestyle has called me to confront questions, to seek answers, to consider at length my value system, my opinions, who I am, and what is and what is not meaningful to me.

I have found satisfaction nestled in my cabin in the woods of southern Indiana with my dog—without television or nearby neighbors. I write letters, walk the forests, occasionally sleep outdoors near the water's edge, swim in my small lake, and tinker in my workshop. Once in a while, when I become concerned that my life is too isolated and detached, I visit the village to enjoy a bowl of the Hobnob's black-bean soup and conversation with a few of the townsfolk. But most important, visits from family and friends have become, as never before, treasured gifts. And to my surprise, my friends have managed to find their way to the door of my remote, backroads, off-the-track haven to visit and to relax.

The Hobo Bunkhouse

There is a bunkhouse behind my cabin on a small, clear lake where hobos sometimes stay. It was there when I bought the property, and it consists of a single room approximately fifteen by eighteen feet. There are five windows looking out in three directions. I furnished it with a table and chairs, a small pantry, and two beds. Books fill the cases of the headboards. *The World Is My Home* by James Michener, *On the Road* by Jack Kerouac, *Blue Highways* by William Least Heat Moon, and *Zen and the Art of Motorcycle Maintenance* by Robert Pirsig are among the choices. The 'bos will sometimes leave one or two behind, adding to the collection. A wooden cigar box atop the pantry holds a deck of cards, stamps, and stationery.

The pantry is kept filled with outdoor cookware, a coffee pot, and basic canned goods: peanut butter, jelly, Spam, soups, coffee, and so forth. I have not hinted in any way that what is used needs to be restocked, but some walk or bike the mile and a half to a country store and purchase replacements before leaving. One visitor left three dollars with a thank-you note.

Many carve names, marks, and messages into the bunkhouse paneling. On the table rests a journal that explains the rules and invites visitors to record any thoughts or feelings that they might like to share with other guests. The first page welcomes the 'bos:

> Welcome, Friends:
>
> Enjoy your stay here. Everything in the hobo bunkhouse is for your use and enjoyment—food, soap, towels, etc.
>
> Sleep, relax, swim, hike, meditate, enjoy the beauty of nature . . . and you will leave here more at peace.
>
> Please don't harm anything. The deer, chipmunks, birds— even the snakes and spiders—are part of nature's delicate balance.
>
> We are only visitors here. Take pleasure in the intricate nature of the spider's web, a doe stretching her neck into the pond for a morning drink, a black snake sunning on a rock, or a turtle creeping through long grass. How precious are these quiet opportunities!
>
> You are invited to share your feelings/insights in this journal (name and date with each entry, please).
>
> May your feet stay loose and your fancy free. Peace.

Cardboard's Jungle

The first June after moving here, I received a postcard from Cardboard. He was planning to jump freights from California to visit me. He would be staying about two weeks in the bunkhouse. Though the bunkhouse rules state a maximum of two nights, I often make exceptions for those who have been hard on the road for a lengthy period of time or who have traveled long stretches. Cardboard was then in his seventies, and a trip of that distance on main lines was one whopping endeavor. Since trains do not pass near Nashville, Indiana, Cardboard would call me when he arrived in Indianapolis or any town nearby, and I would pick him up.

Cardboard is a recluse. Though he generally attended the national convention in Britt, he would always set up his own jungle apart from all the others. He would visit the convention jungle site, talk to the few select hobos he trusted, and rudely shun all others. When he'd had enough of people, or when he became angry at someone, he would slip away into the weeds to his own secluded spot, or stomp off angrily down the tracks threatening never to return.

The first time he saw me, he glanced at my recorder and waved me away indignantly. "I don't want no damn woman reporter prying into my life." I was disappointed. I truly was interested in this man who had made the road his home for more than fifty years, but I assured him I would not attempt to question him. From that moment on, I never went near him with my recorder. By the time I left a week later, he had given me a post office box number in Broderick, California. We wrote several times throughout that year.

It was a literary wonder how many words Cardboard could fit on a postcard. I had to use a magnifying glass on a few occasions to make out the tiny print. "I'm getting more for my money," he once penned in miniature.

When I saw him the next year at Britt, he spoke briefly to me, but kept his distance for the first couple of days. Then one afternoon he walked into the jungle and, waiting until he could speak to me alone, said, "If you want to grab that tape recorder and camera of yours, you can come with me over to my jungle and ask me some of those questions."

I did not waste a second. We walked through the corner of a corn field, past an abandoned shack, and across a half-acre of shoulder-high brush before we came upon a clearing which had been stomped down and layered with several thicknesses of cardboard. He motioned for me to sit down. On the makeshift floor were two cups, two napkins, a jug of water, and a plastic bag of fried chicken. "I have lunch for us," he smiled proudly.

"Cardboard, what a treat this is!" I set up my tape recorder, and he served the chicken and poured us water. For more than two hours, I asked; he answered. He had been born in my hometown of Indianapolis and had done construction work for a builder who lived within blocks of me. We had grown up knowing the same city streets and parks and bus system—though we had known them during different generations.

I felt good about the interview and about the rapport we were finally enjoying. I thanked him: "I can't tell you how much I appreciate the time you've given me and the wonderful information. And the chicken! I sure didn't expect lunch, too!"

He was picking up our trash as he responded, "Can you believe they throw good food like that away?"

"Throw it away?!" I surely sounded as shocked as I felt. "Where did you get it?"

"Outta the dumpster behind Casey's. I watched them pitch it. It was still hot. Now, that's a sin, throwing away good food like that."

Enter Cardboard into my life!

The longer I knew him, the closer we became and the better I understood that this man was truly one of a kind. And now, nearly eight years later, I awaited a phone call from the Avon Yard in Indianapolis. The loner who wouldn't speak to me when we first met was jumping freights cross-country to spend two weeks.

The call came late on a Sunday afternoon. "Cardboard, where are you?" I asked anxiously.

"I'm in goddamn Effingham, Illinois. Been stuck here now for two stinking days. I'm waiting for a train to Indianapolis or Terre Haute, but not a damn thing!"

"Don't move," I told him. "I'm getting in the car right now."

When I arrived in the Effingham Yard five hours later, I

walked past a few buildings, across tracks, through bushes, and finally to a small block utility building. Under some nearby maintenance equipment was a piece of cardboard. On it, sound asleep and layered with dirt, was my old friend.

When we arrived home and Cardboard saw my little bunkhouse, he said, "Oh, man, I'll take to that like stink on shit!" And he did. Creating a hobo jungle behind it on the lake became a mission for him. He worked for days with a shovel, bringing the incline to ground level. He walked the woods, went dumpster diving in town, and "liberated" materials from behind buildings until he had what he needed to complete his task. Each day I returned from work eager to discover what he had built.

Cardboard was driven! He took breaks only to ride with me to Indianapolis to visit his childhood home and his old grade school and to make a three-day trip to Toledo, where a few hobos were gathered. Cardboard's mind was set persistently on his task.

As we were eating dinner one evening beside the lake, he shared his work philosophy. "I always have to stay busy. I like to do my part, to pay my way. If there's anything I hate it's a jungle buzzard! Finishing a job like this one is like being an artist. You dab a little here, dab a little there." He reached into the air with his imaginary brush. "You never quit. Just keep working, just keep dabbing. And sometimes, for the longest time, nothing looks finished until suddenly one day—presto—you have a master-piece!"

Cardboard's jungle was a masterpiece like no other. The fire ring was made of a truck-wheel rim from the local junkyard. Above it was a tripod of heavy hickory branches about two inches in diameter and seven feet long. They were tied at the top with a strip of leather and supported a heavy chain and hook which would hold the stew pot. In the side of a hill he had carved out another fire pit and covered it with a steel grid for coffee pots and gun boats. Large wooden cable spools had been turned into work tables and scrap lumber into benches.

After he completed the final grading and planted grass seed, we were no longer allowed to step foot in that jungle again.

Even during the daily waterings, we stood outside its perimeter. "But Cardboard," I objected, "if we can't go in, you won't get to enjoy the jungle that you worked so hard to build."

"Oh, no, you don't understand," he explained. "I didn't build it for me. I built it for the other guys who'll stop by to use it."

Wayfaring Friends

Indeed, many have stopped by to enjoy Cardboard's jungle and the bunkhouse. They cook over the fire, swim in the lake, leave entries in the journal, and sign their names on the inside walls: "Always wanted my own knothole, Liberty Justice" (on a knotty panel of wood); "Back by popular demand, Midwest"; "Iowa Blackie was here." Hobo marks are also plentiful on the walls and sills. These marks, left by one wayfarer as a message to the next, have long been part of the hobo culture. My favorite is on a telephone pole about thirty feet from my drive. It consists of an X with a line above it and a small circle on both sides. An arrow below it points toward my cabin. That particular mark is just one of hundreds and means "good jungle." It reminds me each time I turn into my drive that Cardboard's jungle has developed a reputation of excellence.

I try to spend quality time with my visitors. Some come here right off the road, weary and dirty. Taking a shower and doing laundry are priorities. Then come the more enjoyable requests. Can we go dumpster diving? Hunting for walking sticks? Hiking? To the thrift stores?

Nearly everyone insists on helping out. Raking leaves, washing my car, cleaning the garage. Once when Road Hog visited after a three-month trek on the road, I woke at dawn to get a drink of water. In the early morning dimness, I thought I saw something move outside my kitchen window near the lake. It was Road Hog atop the bunkhouse with a broom sweeping pine needles from the roof and cleaning the gutters. Before he left a week later, he had washed every window in my cabin. He had also filled a notebook with his personal philosophy. One entry reads:

The happiest hobo in the world is the hobo who has achieved his self-reliance and self-confidence. He is secure on the road knowing that he will be able to meet his basic needs. . . .

Pray for what you want, but work for what you need!

A good hobo should never hang his head down like a tramp or a bum. There is no shame in asking anyone for work to get what you need. An oldtime hobo once told me when one door closes, another one opens. If you get turned down, walk away with a smile and say, "Thank you, Sir" with your head in the air. Sooner or later, in a day's time, a door will open and your needs will be met.

You can always be a Windex Hobo! Invest in a little bottle of cleaner and a roll of paper towels and walk up to small business places and offer to shine their windows for whatever they can afford.

On another occasion, when the town of Nashville asked me to consider putting my cabin on the log home tour, I decided it might be a good opportunity to allow my community to visit the bunkhouse and jungle in order to better understand these characters who were passing through their town occasionally. During the tour weekend, Midwest John, a guitar-picking hobo, stayed in the bunkhouse and joined me in the jungle area both days to greet visitors after they had walked through the cabin and the bunkhouse. We entertained hundreds of small groups of visitors (several thousand people, according to the sorority hostesses who organized the event) with hobo songs and stories. Midwest, as usual, had his old hat on the ground to encourage tips.

Midwest is in his thirties and has lived on the road since he was about fifteen years old, making his way on meager tips from gigs in small bars, honky tonks, and festivals. I had met him five years earlier in a jungle at a railroad festival in Logansport, Indiana. I was confused when I noticed him the next morning beside the fire sewing a patch over a large hole in the crotch of his jeans—while he was wearing them! "Why don't you change into another pair so you can stitch them up more easily?" I asked.

"This is the only pair I own," he explained.

"Well, if you ever throw them away, I'd like to have them." He stared at me in disbelief! "I don't know why, really. Maybe I'll make something out of them." We both laughed at the idea. Two weeks later, he personally delivered them to my front door. We have been friends since.

He wrote a song about our friendship. Each stanza ended "I thank the Lord each passing day I've got a friend like you."

He played that song often during the log home tour, and I wore my overalls covered with a great little denim apron which a friend had made me from Midwest's old jeans. When the event ended late Sunday, he sat down at the large antique chopping block which serves as my kitchen table to count his money, and I excused myself to shower and change. When I came back to the kitchen a half-hour later, there sat my rag-tattered, road-worn, "never-got-more-than-a-buck-to-my-name" friend at my table, which was covered with neat stacks of bills—more than five hundred dollars! With a broad smile, he made up his own parody, singing "Hey, I may be ragged and funny! But I got a barrel of money! I'll just travel along, until it's all gone . . . "

Especially in the summer months, the bunkhouse is a popular haven. Generally at least one or two visitors arrive each month. A few times, groups of hobos have met here for a weekend, cooking stew and playing music. When no one comes around for a while, I need only to go inside and read the walls to recall the special times I've had with Inkman, Ohio Ned, Iowa Blackie, Tramp Printer, Iron Horse Brad, Be Gone Norm, Buckeye Driller, Lake Shore Charlie, Big Skip, Hippie Hobo, and many, many others.

Unquestionably, Cardboard had created a simple hobo masterpiece in the hills of Brown County.

Last June I received a call from a nurse at a hospital in Oroville, California. "I have an older man here who has apparently had a stroke. He isn't able to speak. He doesn't have much identification on him. He just handed me a card from his pocket that says, 'In case of emergency or injury call Gypsy Moon.' The card has your phone number."

Since Cardboard couldn't speak for himself, I flew to California to make sure that he was getting proper care. He had been transferred to a hospital in a neighboring city. On the third day of my visit, I was told that he didn't have insurance and was not cooperating with the therapy departments, and the hospital would no longer keep him.

"What are you going to do with him?" I asked the doctor.

He said, "We can't keep him. I suggest you take him home."

"Home," I said, "is a railroad yard in Oroville."

"Well," the doctor continued coolly, "that's where he'd probably be happiest."

I was livid. "He's lost strength on his right side. He can't talk. He can't write. According to your own speech therapist, he can't even point appropriately to pictures. And you want me to drop him off in a railroad yard? He needs to be in a safe place for at least two months until we see how much he recovers from the stroke. Is that unreasonable?"

The doctor concluded in a monotone, "He has to go."

"If *you* want him dropped off in a railyard," I screamed, "*you* put him in *your* car and *you* do it! He's my friend! Don't ask me to dump him out there with no help! If he were your father, would you turn him out?"

My tantrum was effective. By the time I left California, Cardboard had been placed short-term in a nursing home in Chico. After three weeks, he was released.

Six months later, a nurse called from Seattle, Washington. Cardboard had suffered a second stroke and was in the veterans' hospital there. He was eventually transferred to a long-term care facility. Road Hog, who was in Dunsmuir, California, jumped freights to check on him. They called me from the nursing home.

"Cardboard," I shouted into the mouthpiece, "I'm coming to visit you in a few weeks."

He shocked me when he managed to get a few words out in their proper sequence, a feat he generally could accomplish only when he was angry. "Too fuckin' long! Be dead!"

While I was making arrangements to visit him in hopes of possibly getting him transferred to a facility near me, I was told by the hospital that he had "escaped." Four months later, I learned he had jumped aboard a train somewhere in the L.A. area and had fallen off in Ventura. He was found beside the rails unconscious and with a fractured skull. A week later the nurse informed me by phone, "Your friend is now out of intensive care and has just told the nurses to go to hell!"

Again, Cardboard was fighting to make it clear that he intended to spend the last days of his journey living his life his way—on the road that he had long called home. I pray that with each attempt he encounters gentle people, and that he always finds a jungle as comfortable as the one he created behind my bunkhouse.

A Hard Lesson

I have many fond memories of my cabin and bunkhouse and jungle and a particular appreciation for the comfort and security they provide, so the hardest lesson for me to learn from my hobo friends was that there is a distinct difference between *house* and *home*.

I have long been aware that most of my vagabond visitors have a sort of mysterious, yet solid, deliberate footing as they drift from location to location. Steamtrain explained, "Hobos may be houseless, but they are not homeless; they are at home wherever they wander, wherever they put down their bedroll."

But it was Texas Madman's lesson around a jungle fire one cool autumn morning that I will always remember.

> I just want to make one thing clear. I am *not* homeless. I have a home—a big and beautiful one. In fact, you're sitting in it right now. Under your feet is my bed and over your head is my roof. Granted, the bed may have lumps in it and the roof leaks from time to time, but I wouldn't think of trading this home for any other.

Steamtrain and Madman were saying the same thing in slightly different ways: A house is a building, but home is an attitude—a state of mind that nurtures us, offers us security, and ensures us that though we venture away (or adventure away), home can remain steadfastly within us. *House* is external; *home* is internal.

Internalizing that lesson took time. It is too easy for me to get comfortable, to carry around a security blanket—a sort of quilt pieced together with bits of job security, daily routine, a favorite chair, a bowl of evening popcorn. It feels warm and cozy and snug. Yet my involvement in the hobo community was challenging my comfort zone. I was becoming aware that I could leave my cabin and all that is warm and cozy and comfortable without leaving home at all. I was slowly realizing that security does not come from what is external, like the pieces in the quilt, but rather from what is internal—an attitude, a state of mind, a confidence; a self-assurance; an inner, spiritual peace.

Then one August evening, I finally flung the comforter aside and detached myself from all its predictability for the simple sake of setting myself free.

My First Freight Trip

Britt, Iowa, dispels the myth that all small midwestern farming towns are narrow-minded. On the contrary, this Bible Belt community has played host nearly every August since 1900 to a diverse group of counterculture, vagabond free spirits.

Welcome to the home of the annual National Hobo Convention.

The convention is the highlight of my year. It is both a homecoming and an opportunity to visit with some of my dearest friends, many of whom I see only at this annual event. It is also a chance to meet new people—hobos and other free spirits. Long-time attendees enjoy their role as hosts and work at making sure first-timers feel welcome. Hobos at heart, hobos who have settled down, and rubber tramps (those on the road in an old car) travel here in vehicles; others make their way hitchhiking, walking, and freight jumping.

The town has established a National Hobo Foundation, a not-for-profit organization that funds a local museum on hobo history, the convention site, and a hobo memorial. Though the convention has been held here for more than ninety years, the actual jungle site has shifted over the years from one end of town to another. The site is a permanent one now, donated by the Buss family as a memorial to a relative and town resident who died a couple of years ago. It is located on the edge of town along the old Milwaukee Railroad, now the Soo Line. The foundation collaborated with the hobos to improve ways of meeting the needs of the hundreds of 'bos who show up each year (such as a boxcar for shelter, showers and baths, electricity, and other amenities), and they continue to work together to raise funds for further improvements.

The town's Hobo Days Committee promotes its own festival during the convention weekend, which draws an estimated crowd of 35,000. Visitors (and more reporters than the hobos care to tolerate) enjoy the parade, a flea market, street sales, a car show, a carnival, free mulligan stew, the coronation of the National Hobo King and Queen, and hobnobbing with both oldtime and new-generation hobos in the jungle.

The hobos have a few specific events of their own, which occur toward the end of the week. The musicians among the lot—and there are usually plenty—take an afternoon to perform at the three local nursing homes. On Friday a memorial service is held at the cemetery. A closed hobo community meeting follows, with lively political discussion regarding the rules and bylaws. Candidates for king and queen are interviewed by the council, which is made up of five hobos selected by the community. Those whom the council considers qualified according to the bylaws are put on a slate to run. Before the Saturday election, a hobo parade features nearly as many of the townspeople participating as watching. The parade is followed by a hobo auction on the town square to raise funds for the Hobo Foundation. Collectors, tourists, and townsfolk bid on items belonging to and made by the hobos. Then comes the election, with every hobo campaigning for a favorite candidate. Afterward is the finale—the coronation of the new king and queen.

While each 'bo has his own favorite event, the memorial service at Britt's Evergreen Cemetery is attended by nearly one hundred percent of them. It is symbolic and meaningful. All dress in their most decorative garb and bring their walking sticks. Hobos who have died during the year can be cremated. Their ashes, which have been held by the local mortician, are laid to rest by their brothers and sisters at this ceremony. The service begins with Songbird singing the National Anthem. Steamtrain Maury, Minneapolis Skinny, and hobo chaplain Father John Brickley, now in his eighties, preside.

While the local color guards stand at attention, the symbolism in the memorial is explained. The large railroad-tie cross represents the hobos' strong ties to the railroad. The burlap draped over the arms of the cross symbolizes humility. The grapevine wreath in the center is a reminder of hardships endured on the road. The bouquets of wildflowers scattered about remind us that God will provide for our needs, just as He cares for the lilies of the field. The sections of split-rail fence with a hoe propped in one corner reaffirm that hobos are workers. A bronze plaque at the foot of the cross bears these words: "National Hobo Memorial . . . dedicated to those free-spirited men and women whose migratory work patterns helped meet the labor needs of America from the Civil War to the Great Depression."

Bandanas are spread over each marker. The hobos, their shoulders also draped with burlap, circle the various stones with walking sticks outstretched. The community believes that walking sticks possess special powers, because many of God's miracles were performed not by human hands but by a walking stick—the water that sprang from a rock or the rod that turned to a serpent. Finally, a few drops of Irish whiskey are poured on each grave. However, Mountain Dew, one of those buried there, never drank whiskey, so a can of Mountain Dew is dribbled his way. Frisco Jack reads the names from the long list of hobos who have "caught the westbound" (whether buried in Britt or not), and Harmonica Mike plays the sound of a steam whistle after each name is read. After a couple of favorite hobo songs by various musicians, Luther the Jet ends by singing a piece that he wrote titled "Hobos' Remembrance" that includes the monikers of those laid to rest there.

Most of this hoopla occurs on Friday and Saturday. The earlier part of the week is filled with more intimate yet diverse activity. The center of the hubbub is the kitchen, located off to the far side of the jungle and equipped with a number of large makeshift tables and a refrigerator. (The town ran electricity to us several years ago.) A couple of fires are kept going from daybreak until after dinner. A group is always busy peeling, chopping, mixing, and stirring. It is not unusual to serve a couple hundred at an evening meal, so the preparation begins early. Breakfast is served daily, and the menu depends on what is on hand—chicken and noodles, spaghetti, or hobo stew. On one occasion, Steamtrain Maury asked me to accompany him to a nearby farm, where he talked the lady of the house into supplying enough buffalo meat to feed two hundred hungry vagabonds.

Steamtrain Maury, in his late seventies, is the chief organizer (though since his stroke in 1991, he has become a master at delegating), and he is considered the hobos' elder statesman. He explains the symbolism as the community fire is lit at the beginning of the week. The younger 'bos are committed to keeping it burning until after the last event, a hobo poetry reading, on Sunday morning.

Throughout other areas of the jungle, little groups are huddled together here and there in intimate discussions about railroads, towns where work is plentiful, or the good old days. Jam sessions throughout the afternoon draw little clusters of foot tappers.

The more enterprising are busy creating traditional hobo art items to exchange with friends, to sell, or to donate to the auction. The Texas Madman is famous for his bits of wisdom stitched onto scraps of denim. Frisco Jack, Cinderbox Cindy, Be Gone Norm, Knotman, and Spike make leather monkey's-fist necklaces, which express community. Liberty Justice, Big Skip, and Iron Horse Brad whittle and carve walking sticks or pieces of worm-eaten bark from the woodpile. Minneapolis Jewel heaps a picnic basket—which annually brings record bids during the auction—full of her homemade jams, breads, candies, and jerky. And there are always a few roustabouts from the previous night stretched out under a tree on pieces of cardboard. Local farmers sometimes bring in a tub of sweet corn, which is boiled up midafternoon, and if we're lucky, a pound of butter is set out and used up before the summer sun can melt it.

In the evenings, hundreds of townsfolk and out-of-town visitors join us and are told that when the light of the jungle fire shines on their faces, they are a part of the hobo community. They consider it an invitation to join in the music, stories, poetry, and the ever-popular hobo shuffle, danced by young and old alike in a circle around the fire. Connecticut Shorty, New York Maggie, Road Hog, and the Sidedoor Pullman Kid surprisingly encourage even the shyest to shift from onlooker to participant.

With the exception of an occasional squabble, the atmosphere is warm and friendly—and somewhat surreal, like stepping into a small midwestern farm town in the 1920s just before harvest. Hobos and hobos and more hobos hanging out in jungles near the tracks and waiting until the crops are ready to come in.

The hobos who come to Britt, like nearly all hobos in the past, have used monikers. Since many of them ran away from home at an early age, and because freight jumping is illegal, aliases are useful to avoid being tracked down. Also, a road name tells something about the 'bo. Steamtrain Maury is a natural leader; Reefer Charlie preferred riding fast, high-priority trains that carried perishables in refrigerated cars called reefers; and Gas Can Paddy carried his personal belongings in a modified gas can because he was more likely to be picked up when he hitchhiked. Names such as Eastcoast Charlie, New York Ron, and Santa Fe Bo hint at the region where the hobo grew up or traveled. Connecticut Shorty's title combines a reference to her height with her father's name, Connecticut Slim. Generally, monikers were given to hobos by their fellow vagabonds. In many cases, being given a name was a sort of rite of passage. When a young man was no longer considered a greenhorn by the older 'bos, the elders would "knight" him with a road name.

Being dubbed with a road name is an honor—in my case, one I never tire of recalling. I had given considerable thought to joining one of my friends on a freight ride but had simply not been invited. Most hobos, I have found, are reluctant to allow a woman to accompany them. Maybe they are concerned about the impropriety, or perhaps they simply feel—as they do about traveling with any greenhorn—that a woman might slow them down. Late one Thursday evening during the convention, after all the singing and tales had died down with the fire, a few hobos strolled into one of the town's three watering holes. I joined them. The Pole Inn is about a mile walk from the jungle site along a country road that borders the tracks.

After an hour or so, I decided to head back to the fire to get a good night's sleep before the big events of the following day. Friday of convention week is packed with activity, and I was already overtired from sitting up until two o'clock the previous morning watching a remarkable meteor shower which, according to astronomers, was to continue two more days.

A few of us slept down the tracks that night, away from the town lights, to enjoy nature's free exhibition. Lying on our backs, we watched shooting star after shooting star streak across the clear night sky. The oldtimers had legends to share.

"After hobos die, they ride the tail of Halley's Comet to heaven," Steamtrain began. He continued, like Old Great-Grandfather Storyteller, to explain that since the comet comes around only once every seventy-six years, quite an assemblage of free spirits are gathered to climb aboard for the next ethereal ride. I listened with interest as Ramblin' Rudy, Alabama, and Charlie Tuna speculated that heaven is simply a celestial jungle with trains that come and go on time, no bulls, and plenty of stew.

Man-Called-John headed off on another bit of stellar lore, talking at length about how few hobos can claim to ever have seen a shooting star cross the path of the moon. The occurrence is so very rare that it is believed that the moon casts a spell on any who witness it. The moon becomes, for those chosen few, a "Gypsy moon," instilling in them an insatiable appetite to wander.

I was recalling these tales as I got up to leave the Pole Inn. One among us, Snapshot, said, "Wait a minute, Jackie, I'll walk back to the jungle with you." We paid for our drinks and had started down the country road when Snapshot stopped. "I hear a train coming from the east."

I expressed my disappointment that we weren't already back at the jungle. I have always loved seeing the oldtimers, many with long white beards and walking sticks, shuffle to the track as the train approaches to pay homage to the era they so fondly remember. They wave, and the engineer generally obliges with a long, lonesome wail on the whistle.

"Well," said my friend, hoping to make me feel less cheated, "we can pay our respects right here."

We walked across the road and waited beside the track. We waved our arms, watching the train bear down on us. What power! My heart raced as the ground trembled underfoot. Then, the engines having passed, the steady rhythm mesmerized me as car after car blurred by.

Snapshot broke the spell. "Jackie, you've said you'd like to jump a freight. This one's going pretty slow."

It sure looked much too fast for me! Snapshot encouraged me to step back into the road for a clearer perspective. From some distance now, I could judge that it was moving quite slowly.

"Snapshot," I reasoned apologetically, "I've always told myself I would never get on a moving freight. It's just too risky."

He spoke genuinely, "I sure don't want to talk you into doing anything you're not comfortable with."

A gentle sort, a thinker and a philosopher, Snapshot spends much of his time reading and discussing what he has read.

He is fiftyish, wears thick glasses, is slight of build, has a short, neatly trimmed beard, and wears a beret that hangs to the right of his head. When I first met him, he reminded me of an artist. When he is not on the road, he stays in an old school bus on a secluded piece of wooded property in Florida. The last few years he has been in his bus more than he's been on the road. Much of what he eats comes from the forests: game, berries, plants, and teas. He earns his living for the most part buying and selling anything from junk to treasures. He is proficient with a camera (hence his name), and has worked on the road as a chef. Once, in a letter to me, he wrote:

> I'm often asked, "What is a hobo?" I'm not sure I know the answer—yet I can't just accept some glib characterization. For a hobo is a complex individual who has broken the mold into which society would force him. He has sprouted wings, although they're somewhat tattered from his travels. A hobo is on a first name basis with heat and cold, hunger and thirst, danger, exhaustion, pain and loneliness—but also love.

We walked back near the tracks and continued watching our train. "This is what the hobos call 'scoping the drag'— watching a train for a good ride," he explained.

To our surprise, at that very moment the train stopped. Directly in front of us was a grain car with a porch, one of the few good rides on the train. Snapshot held out his hand like a valet at the Park Plaza: "Your car, Madam."

It was a moment of decision. I looked at the can of pop that I still held in my hand, then ceremoniously flung it into the high grass. Snapshot, obviously taken aback by my gesture, likewise flung his bottle of beer. We climbed aboard just seconds before the train departed. Our other hobo friends had stepped out the door of the Pole Inn and were shouting farewells to us as we rolled out of Britt and into the warm, black summer night.

"Snapshot," I asked, "where are we going?"

"I don't know," he answered. "If we were moving the

other direction, I would say to Mason City, but I've never ridden west of Britt to find out what's there."

"How far will the train go before it stops?" I persisted.

"Well," he began nonchalantly, "it's just hard to tell. If it's a local, it may stop at every grain elevator along the way. Then again, hell, we could end up in Nebraska."

"Nebraska!" I gasped in a panic. "How are we going to get back to the jungle after we do get off?"

Snapshot didn't answer my question. Instead he became the philosopher that I had always admired. "Jackie, whatever concerns you have right now, you will still have when our trip has ended. Worrying can't change them, so I suggest that we put them on hold until our ride is over. Right now, just try to relax and enjoy the ride."

That was my most memorable lesson in hobo philosophy.

A deep peace, an internal sense of home, replaced my anxiety. Leaning back against the cool, rocking steel of our car, I took a deep breath of the Iowa night, rich with pungent odors of cattle and soil and wheat. I listened as my bearded sage and fellow freight-jumper taught me how to get comfortable on a grainer and how to enjoy the unknown. Some experiences are magic. Our slowly moving train could have been Halley's Comet carrying us through the Milky Way.

"Life is a journey," Snapshot said, "and we are the travelers." We shrieked and pointed heavenward each time we saw a meteor blaze above us.

When our train stopped thirty minutes later, we were only at the next grain elevator, but during our three-hour walk back, I felt as though I were in the next galaxy, or maybe seventh heaven. I had jumped my first freight, and, if only for a slow, thirty-minute ride, I had thrown my comforter aside; I had sprouted wings; it had been my rite of passage! I had no idea then that this rail trip, albeit short and sweet, was a prelude to years of increasingly long and adventurous ones.

A hearty bunch of inebriated hobos (or should I call them bums?) were still up when we entered the jungle after 4:00 A.M.

I had always been the listener when it came to hobo tales, but tonight I sat by the jungle fire and told them the story of my first freight ride.

The next afternoon, Snapshot and I walked back to the spot where we had boarded and searched for his beer bottle. He signed and dated it. Today it sits on my bookshelf as a reminder that home is in the heart and to just relax and enjoy the ride.

About a week after I returned home from that trip, I received a telegram:

WE RECEIVED CONFIRMATION. YOUR FIRST FREIGHT. CONGRATULATIONS. BE YE KNOWN, HENCEFORTH, AS GYPSY MOON.

It was signed RAILRIDERS OF AMERICA.

My involvement in the community, specifically my role as a Queen, the constant stream of unconventional visitors to my bunkhouse in Brown County, and my numerous railriding trips following the first one with Snapshot, provided me with steady opportunities to record the stories of some remarkable characters. The interviews which I conducted since 1985 opened a door for me. I entered carrying my tape recorder and steno pad, and departed leaving my heart behind. The hobo oral history project— by some brilliant academic magic—turned my father's memories and the recollections of other hobos into research. My father would smile at that!

The American hobo, as we knew him before the 1940s, is fading into memory. As one oldtimer commented, "There are only a handful of us left." And, indeed, only a precious few of these old boxcar barnacles are left to reminisce about the warmth of a jungle fire, the thrill of jumping a rattler, or the satisfaction of evading a railroad dick. The remaining few are willing, even eager, to share their recollections. Their dwindling number makes their stories precious and brings urgency to the task of recording them. Perhaps their accounts are embellished at times or clouded a bit by the span of years, but they remain—for a short time, at least—as a final connection to their rich and scattered legacy. As

Hobo Bob said, "It's done and been."

The settings for the interviews varied, as did my relationships with the interviewees. Some subjects have become my
dearest friends, while I have not seen or spoken with others since
the tapings. Some were recorded beside jungle fires and railroad
tracks, and others in the cozy abodes of oldtimers long ago
married and settled down.

The portions of selected interviews compiled here have
been cautiously edited. Excessive habitual phrases, such as "you
know," have been removed, as have other repetitious or redun-
dant remarks. Occasionally, the chronology of events has been
reorganized into a sequence easier for the reader to follow. Words
or phrases have been added in some cases for clarity; they are
enclosed in brackets [ ].

2

Rail Tales: Oral Histories of American Hobos

Steamtrain Maury

Steamtrain Maury was born in 1917. He was elected National King of the Hobos five times.

At first, I just went in the summertime. I was just a teenage boy then. I got acquainted with a lot of the old men in those days. A lot of people think hoboing originated during that time, but of course it didn't. Hoboing started after the Civil War. The original hobos were all veterans of the Civil War. And after World War I, big numbers hit the road.

They were veterans coming home from the war. A lot of them were still on the road when the Great Depression hit in the 1930s. During the Depression years, thousands of men hit the road and went out looking for work when there wasn't any work. They were just restless men, unemployed. They'd pick up a little work in the harvest fields. That was about all they found during the Depression. There was about a thousand men for every job. They just roamed the country on freight trains and slept out along the rivers. They did chores for something to eat, either for housewives or restaurants. A lot of them lived off the land. Some hunted and fished and ate greens.

I was born in '17. I was thirteen the first year I hit the road, in 1930. I went again in the summer when I was fourteen, went in the summer when I was fifteen. Then I went on the road for three or four years, just staying on the road, finding work here and there.

My dad lived in Toledo. My mother died when I was about twelve. My dad didn't like what I was doing very well, but he didn't do anything about it either. I had a brother and two sisters, but they all were much older than I was. I was the youngest of the family. They were all married and had families by then.

Part of my boyhood, I'd been raised in Idaho. I'd come to Toledo to live with my dad, and I wanted to go back to Idaho where I had been raised the early part of my boyhood. I was set to go back there, and the only way to get there was ride the freight trains.

At first I spent summers in the western states working. I listened to a lot of the oldtime hobos. I listened very carefully to them. They handed me down their histories. At that time those men were in their sixties, seventies, some of them in their eighties. That's how I learned about the oldtime history. There I was a young lad, and I was getting acquainted and listening to all the oldtime hobos that had come from way back before the turn of the century. And I felt like a historian from the very beginning.

In the '30s I stopped hoboing because I got to working steadily and got married. Then later on in life I got crippled up and couldn't work anymore. I was too young to retire. I was only about fifty, and I got hoboing again. Just a little bit at first, and then more and more and more. Finally ended up spending another ten years hoboing—1971 to '80, something like that. I had a wife at home. She was working. She got mad about that. It took a lot of sweet-talking to get back home.

A hobo is a man that worked along the way. People argue about this, but this is the way it was handed down to me. I knew them from back in the old times. The hobos were men that followed the railroads, and they worked here and there. They all had a trade or craft to work at. The tramps were a group of men that also came out of the services of the army, but they were men that walked wherever they went. The word *tramp* means "walker." "Tramp, Tramp, Tramp, the Boys Are Marching." Remember that old song? Tramp, tramp, meant marching in the service. A professional walking man, he was called a tramp. And he worked. A lot of people argue about that too, but a tramp does do work. He was just a different kind of vagabond than a hobo.

Another difference is hobos were clannish, they were a brotherhood, and they rode the freight trains. They were organized, they had conventions, they had leaders, district leaders, and they had national leaders. It was like that then, and it still is today. The hobos still have a convention every year in Britt, Iowa. It's been held there for eighty-five years. I was elected the hobo king five different times.

They was in Chicago before they moved to Iowa at the turn of the century. In the year 1900 they wanted to change because Chicago was getting to be such a large city. People would throw rocks at them, and there were big crowds gathering around too much. Sometimes the police would bother them. They wanted to get away from that big crowd, that big city. They wanted to get in a small community, someplace centrally located. Britt, Iowa, was a little town out on the prairie. They said, "Let's invite them out here." And they did. Some of the kings and some of the leaders of the hobos went out there, and they had a meeting. They decided to start having the convention there that year. They met just periodically from then on for twenty years. They didn't have a yearly convention, but it was their headquarters. They would have meetings there and small gatherings. Then in 1933 they started having regular national conventions every year. They also held regional meetings.

Now, there's an early conception about how the word *hobo* began. It has to do with these fellows around the turn of the century that used to carry a hoe with them. They would make a living with a hoe. Every woman in town had a garden, and all the farmers had gardens, and the field also had to be worked with a hoe. And a lot of the oldtime hobos carried their own hoes with them. People would say, "There goes a hobo, a traveling man with a hoe, a 'hoe boy.'"

They might be called a boy. But men, they'd say, "Hey, I'm a man, you speak to me as a man." So they called him "bo." A "bo" is a man, an adult. They called them "ho bo." And that's where the name started.

There was even a few women during the Depression years. Women that hoboed. Boxcar Bertha was one. She retired and lived in Burlington, Iowa, for quite a while. Died about five years ago. She wrote a book [*Boxcar Bertha, An Autobiography, as told to Ben L. Reitman,* with an introduction by Kathy Racker].

Very few of them that I ever heard of did it out of necessity. They did it because they wanted a free life. You know, street people that are on the streets today, thousands of homeless street people, they're out there because of necessity. They're out there because they can't make it. But hobos were not like that in any way. They were men that left home and chose that kind of life.

There never was any bums among us. A bum is a person that can't make it, won't make it. A bum is a local person around town that won't work or can't work, maybe even handicapped. Doesn't travel unless it's just down to the next town. Now, there's been some bums that got out and traveled around, a little of them up and down the coast or someplace. But bums are usually alcoholics or men that can't work, or won't work. But the hobos all had good trades and good arts and crafts that they worked at. And they made their way. They didn't bum their way.

I have seen whole families on the road—riding the freight trains, working and picking fruit, working in the harvest fields. And women were safe in those days. I can remember one woman who got in a boxcar with twenty-five men, and nobody even thought about bothering her—not one. Now, that wouldn't happen today. But it was that way back in the '30s. And they were just as safe out there as they would have been at home. Most of the men worried about them, thought they shouldn't be out there.

They didn't see that as a life for a woman. And there wasn't a lot of them, just very, very few of them.

When you weren't on freights, the jungles were your home. You stayed in the jungle camps. Men would go out in all different directions and come in with vegetables, meat, and things to throw in the stew. They would make a big old stew, and they'd always hunt wild animals, and they'd fish. They'd wash their clothes; the hobos kept themselves clean. A lot of times the jungles were located near rivers or creeks. Near rivers or a place where there was plenty of water so that they could wash clothes and cook—and they could fish a lot, too. A lot of the hobos were good at living off the land. They knew all the wild food to eat.

A lot of men got out on the road during the Depression because they didn't have no place to live. They'd leave home because they had to. A lot of men went out on the road because they were dropouts, they couldn't make it. But hobos weren't dropouts. Hobos chose their lives because they wanted adventures, outdoor life.

You know what's important to a hobo, really important? Letters. Lots of rambling folks got a mail drop—someplace where they can get mail when they pass that way. I wrote thousands of letters when I was on the road. And it was so important to get them, too. One of my closest friends for life is a rambling man from Sydney, Australia. Never met the man—probably never will—but we've written for many, many years. 'Course, I'll meet him by the river, the river Jordan. Letters is one way that hobos draw close, into a family, into a tribe. And now that so many of us are old and off the road, it's through letters that our community stays strong and connected.

Back in the '30s, I'd look for work. I had been raised on farms and ranches, and I could do farm work and use a team of horses. That's the kind of work I'd look for. And if I couldn't find work, I'd be traveling on down to another location pretty fast. I just traveled the country and found work where I could. I got into construction work, stayed there for a while, and then moved on to another place. The whole time by train. Did a lot of walking, too.

The railroad personnel didn't like it. They didn't like it at all. There's always been a hard time riding the freight trains. The railroad policemen try to keep you off. But the hobos always felt they were part of the railroad, and a lot of the hobos had been railroad men. They worked on the railroads—a lot of them did. Some [railroad men] were very friendly, and the years that I spent on the road a lot of the railroad men became my personal friends and helped me in every way they could to keep me safe, because the railroad's an awfully dangerous place to be. It's so dangerous that most people just don't ride anymore.

I've seen a lot of people get hurt on the railroads. The hobos never got hurt so much, because they were experienced, and they knew all the safety rules, and they abided by them. But a lot of greenhorns, guys just going out. Like during the '30s, thousands of men hit the road, and they didn't know anything about railroads. A lot of those men got hurt. A lot of them got killed. I've seen a lot of them get hurt. When they would start to get off the train when it was coming in the yard, they'd jump off that train when it was still moving real fast, and they would slide hand over feet, break limbs. They would get cinders in their knees, in their foreheads, in their elbows, in their mouths. They'd just get badly hurt. Some guys fall under the wheels, get their legs cut off. Getting on and off trains is extremely dangerous.

The railroad police were there to keep you off the trains. And during the '30s they'd shoot you off. They shot at me in Louisville and several other cities that I've rode through. I was very fortunate. I've never got hit, but I've seen other men get shot. And I've seen men who railroad police beat half to death. A man I rode with a couple of times got beat up real bad. The railroad police would do that if they could catch them. Beat them up bad. A lot of men were jailed for riding freight trains. Any man who ever rode a freight train any amount of time got put in jail either for a few days to a few months.

It happened to me many times. There in the '30s, I got put in jail for riding a freight train in Texas. I hate to go back and name specific places, because I don't want to stir up any old troubles.

But in Texas, Kansas, Oklahoma, in Idaho. Usually two or three days. I did fifteen days one time in a place. I did seven days in another place. Men that rode freight trains for any amount of time would go to jail. There were men who were beaten and are still alive to talk about it. You can still get beat and into trouble jumping freights. There's lots of times when you're in danger—when you get in fights with other men, or when the police are after you riding. Any time you ever get in a fight with another man, there's danger.

It was just a dangerous life, but it was a good life, and an adventurous life. A free life. A totally free life.

Alabama Hobo

Alabama Hobo was born in 1915. He was elected National King of the Hobos in 1989.

I was known as the Alabama Hobo back in the '30s. I started hoboing in 1932. I never have given it much thought about why I did it, but I think the main reason was because after the death of my parents, I was upset and didn't know how or what to do with myself. I wanted to see what this old world looked like, so I started hoboing. When I started, I was seventeen years old. I had quit school and didn't finish my education for a number of years after. I was living with my older brother. I had two brothers and two sisters, and they had lives of their own, didn't seem to fill the place of my parents. A couple of my friends talked me into it, and I went on my first hobo trip.

One time out in western Louisiana or eastern Texas, I was in a jungle sitting around a fire. I kept looking at one fellow, because he seemed to be familiar to me. I thought I had seen him before. I finally went over and talked to him, and I found out he was a friend of mine who had gone to junior high school with me. We sat around and talked about what had happened since we had

seen one another last and our families and everything. That was
a real enjoyable moment.

Sometimes it wasn't so enjoyable. I felt hungry many
times when I was out on the road. But only one time did I go
without food for any great length of time, and that was on my first
hobo trip. My two friends told me that if I would go with them,
they had some money. So we got to Chattanooga, and we found
us a place to camp. They went up to the store and bought two cans
of pork and beans and two loaves of bread. We ate pork and beans
and bread that night, and the next morning they got up before I
did, and they went out and found them something to eat. They
said they'd bummed it, and if I wanted anything, I'd have to bum
it, too. Well, I'd never bummed anything in my life. I didn't even
know how. So I didn't get anything to eat that morning. At
lunchtime I didn't get anything, and in the meantime we had
caught a train on the Central Georgia Railroad out of Chattanooga, and got off at a place—I think it was called Bremen,
Georgia. It was a little after lunch, and they went out again. They
bummed them something to eat and came back and was eating
right before me. I was so hungry I felt like taking it away from
them, but I didn't. I decided I would try bumming.

I went up to a house and knocked on the door. A woman
came to the door. I lost my nerve, I just asked her what time it
was—like time meant anything to me, which it didn't. Anyway,
she went back in the house and then came back and told me what
time it was. When I left the house, I was disgusted with myself.

So when I came to another house, I went up to the door,
and I knocked. When the woman came to the door, I kind of lost
my nerve. I just asked for a match. I didn't need a match, but
anyway I was making some progress. So she went back into the
house and got a couple of matches and came to the door and gave
them to me. I got to thinking to myself that if I didn't get
something to eat, I was going to starve.

So the next house I went up to, I was determined that I
was going to ask for something to eat even if I dropped dead. So
when the woman came to the door, I asked her for something to

eat. She said, "Well, son, I don't have anything right now, but I'm stewing some potatoes for lunch. I'll go in there and make you a couple of sandwiches." She went in and made me a couple of sandwiches and mashed potatoes and put a generous portion of butter on it. She brought it back to the door and handed it to me. I was so hungry, I couldn't wait until I got off her porch. I started eating right then. I guess I looked like a hungry hound dog eating a piece of meat. After that I decided I'd never go hungry that long again. If I didn't have any money, I would bum something to eat. So that was my first experience at bumming, and I never have gone hungry any great length of time since then.

I remember transient camps that were established by the U.S. government back in the Depression years, and their purpose was to try to keep the hobos and the transients off the road. All the transient camps that I know about were army bases, naval bases that had been deactivated since World War I. One of them was at Fort Morgan across Mobile Bay from Mobile, Alabama. That was the first one that I was in. I suppose they had them all along the coast. I don't know if they had any inland or not.

They had an office in town, and you could go there and register, and they would take you out to the transient camp. When you got there, you were assigned a bunk and barrack, and each person had light duties to do about four hours a day: clean up the grounds, clean up the barracks, cooking, serving the food, doing KP, working in the office. And they had a little commissary there. Some of them worked in the commissary. You'd have about four hours' duty a day. Then after that, you were off duty and could enjoy going swimming at the beach, fishing off the wharf, the pier, or playing games in the day room—checkers, pool, and card games. They didn't allow any gambling, although occasionally you would see some gambling, but it was not allowed. Against the rules.

It was a pretty good life. They had three good meals a day, and if you needed some shoes, trousers, shirts, or underwear, you could go to the office and make application, and in a day or two they would take you over to Mobile to a store and buy you some shoes or whatever clothing you needed. If you needed a haircut, they paid for your haircut. In my case, I got a pair of trousers. My shoes were in pretty good shape, just the soles were worn. They took me to a shoe shop and had new half-soles and heels put on my shoes. Then they'd take you back to the camp. It was a pretty good life.

It wasn't like army life or anything, wasn't a lot of discipline. They didn't allow any weapons of any kind. If they caught you with any, why, they would take them away from you and put them in the office and keep them until you left. Then when you got ready to leave, they would take you to Mobile and buy you a bus ticket to your hometown. They didn't hand you this ticket. They would put you on the bus and give the ticket to the bus driver. That way they'd keep anybody from maybe selling their ticket and staying on the road. But in the meantime, they paid you fifteen cents a day. That was not much money, but it would buy you bare necessities—razor blades, shaving lotion, things like that. It was a pretty good life. I don't know how many transient camps there were over the nation, but I've heard of a number of them. I finally told them I wanted to go home, so they took me to town, bought me a bus ticket, put me on the bus, and I went home. After I got home, I felt like I'd been on a two-week vacation in Florida! It was pretty nice.

I don't know how long the transient camps were in operation, but I do know that they were in existence a couple of years. Maybe the government realized it wasn't doing any good. There still was just as many on the road as before. There are very few hobos I've ever known that talked about transient camps.

Sometimes the hobos stayed in the missions. That was a place that was supported by some religious group. They furnished a place for you to eat, a place for you to sleep. You had showers, and they'd feed you two meals a day. Wasn't very good meals, but it was enough to exist on. They wouldn't take anybody in that was drinking, and you were not allowed to drink on the premises. You usually had to listen to a sermon every night. Most of the hobos didn't care for that, so they'd go to a Sally.

A Sally is just short for Salvation Army. Back in the Depression, almost every town had a Salvation Army. A town of any size. I stayed in quite a few Salvation Army places. You could go there and register, and they'd take name, age, hometown, and all that stuff. They had showers, and all the Salvation Armies I stayed in had cots. You had a special place assigned to you to sleep. And some of them would feed a meal at night. I think almost all of them fed a meal in the morning. It was usually oatmeal and a day-old roll and coffee. It was a light breakfast, but it would kind of make you feel like you'd had breakfast. The Salvation Army was kind to the ones that came there to spend the night. Most of them would have a limit, some of them one night, some of them three nights. You couldn't stay there week in and week out. You might go off and stay a week and come back and spend another two or three nights there.

A few times I have gone to the jail or city hall and asked them if I could sleep there if the weather was pretty cold or something. Most of the time they'd let me. They'd always take my valuables and put them in a big envelope and keep them for me 'til morning. Then you could leave, or they'd put you in a cell for the night, and sometimes they would feed you breakfast. [Some refer to these one-night jail stays as "courtesy calls."]

They also had flophouses back then. Flophouses. The few that I stayed in, I didn't care too much for. They weren't kept up good. And occasionally you might catch lice, body lice. You could usually get a place to flop for a dime. And most flophouses didn't have any meals. You could stay there I guess as long as you wanted to, long as you had a dime a night. Some of them might have been more than that. In Chattanooga, Judge Fleming, on Ninth and Plum Street, had one that was fairly decent. It was a dime. You could stay there for a dime. Just a place to sleep, you know, and sometimes they'd have a shower. But the flophouses, Salvation Army, and missions was places where you could stay if you weren't around a jungle.

Hobos did a lot of work in helping to build the railroads, dams, and big buildings. Most people just lump all the tramps and bums and winos and hobos together. They consider them as one group of people, but there's some difference. Hobos, generally speaking—'course, they're like any other segment of our society, there's good and there's bad—but most hobos had a trade, and they were proud of their trade. When they were building the first railroads from the East to the West, most of the laborers in the West were Chinese, and in the East most of them were hobos.

There were all kinds of craftsmen in hobos. If they couldn't find a job following their trade, they'd follow the harvest, the wheat field, the potato harvest, the fruit harvest, and sometimes in Florida they would pick oranges. In some other states there would be apple pickers, cherry pickers. Hobos would usually work, but they didn't stay in one place long. They just had a wanderlust, and they wanted to satisfy it.

But there's one thing I would like people to get into their mind: a hobo is a drifting worker. Follows his trade, and if he can't get a job at his trade, he does other work. But a bum, he's just a bum. Wouldn't work if he had a job. And a wino, of course, all he wants is just a little money to buy another bottle. Hobos just worked and rode the trains.

"Hotshot," "manifest," and "local." Those are names that hobos used to describe certain kinds of trains. A hotshot is one that don't stop at every little pigtrail to do any switching or anything like that. It's a through freight. If you take the hotshot, you can make good time on it. And a manifest is a hotshot, too. But it has a more valuable cargo or something that's got to be moved over the rails in the shortest length of time. A manifest is carrying something other than just ordinary freight. And when you catch a manifest, you can be sure that if a railroad dick doesn't put you off, you got it made to the next town. A local is a train that stops at just every little town. Maybe he has a couple of cars to switch out at one town and then picks up a car, then on down at the next town he's got to stop and leave a car and pick up one. It might take you six or seven hours to travel a hundred miles riding a local. Then, of course, there's your passenger train. After I hoboed a lot, I could see the advantages of riding a passenger train. A passenger train will get you there quick, too.

My first hobo trip, these two guys I went off with were going to teach me how to blind a passenger. Blinding is riding the two flexible blinds between the coaches. Most of them refer to riding the blinds right behind the coal tender and the baggage car. Anyway, the blinds is where most of them ride on a passenger train. You're apt to get caught, because you have to wait 'til the passenger train gets into the station before it slows down enough for you to get off. Then you run the risk of getting caught by some security officer, railroad dick, or policeman. But if you can catch one, you can usually make good time. Most freights go in a hole for a passenger. Now, that's a term used for a freight going on a side track to let a passenger train by. In most cases, the passenger train has the right of way. The freight has to go in the hole or on the side track to let them by. And about the only time I know of that a passenger train would opt to go in a hole would be for some manifest that was carrying valuables or highly perishable food.

I have ridden a different way. When the conductor lets the platform down at the door, then he closes the gate, there's room enough under that platform that you can get on the step and draw your legs up and you can ride there. But the hip that's sticking out a little bit takes a beating sometimes, because the suction of the air that the wheels make will throw up small gravel. A lot of it will hit you on the hip. It's not the most comfortable ride, but if I had to go somewhere and that's the only way, why then I'd ride it—but very few times. Most of the times, I got on the blinds.

There were lots of different kinds of cars. First we'll take the old common boxcar. A boxcar has got sides, ends, top, and on each side it has a sliding door. You can get in this boxcar, close the doors, and protect you and your stuff from the weather.

There is the gondola. It's a car that has ends and a side but no top. It's usually about four or five feet high, sometimes six feet high. But it is used to haul pipes, trusses, steel, lumber—things of that nature—that won't be hurt by being exposed to the weather. But riding in a gondola car is very dangerous for a hobo if it has cargo in it. If there is space between what's in the car and the end of the car, some hobos would get down in that. It does seem to be a nice place to ride, but if a train has to go into an emergency stop or a fast stop of any kind, the load is apt to shift forward, and if you're between the wall and the load, why, you'd be crushed to death. So it's better not to ever ride in a gondola when it's loaded.

Next is a grain car. It's a hopper kind of a car used to haul wheat, corn, and other grain. It has—most have—an opening at the top where they can load the grain out of the elevators or conveyors. On the bottom, they usually have about two gates. It's V-shaped, and there's a door on each side of the V. They can crank these out to unload the car. The gates will open, and they usually unload it over some grating or something, so the grain goes down in a storage area.

Then you have a coal car. It has an end and a side. On the bottom, it's shaped similar to the grain car. It has two openings down there—V-shaped—and gates on each side of the V which can be opened when they want to unload the coal. It's not suitable for a hobo to ride in.

Another car is a tanker. They use it to haul chemicals, oil, and liquid stuff. They just usually load it from the top through a round hole that has a lid. They have outlets underneath there, so they can connect hose or pipe when they want to unload it. It's not a good ride.

Then we have a flatcar. It doesn't have any ends or sides. Just a flat bed. It's used to haul flat stuff mostly and stuff that can be fastened down to where it won't shift off the car.

Refrigerator cars are called reefers. The old refrigerator cars had two ice compartments at each end of the car. I don't recall just how big these were, but they took up the width of a boxcar, and then they were about four feet the other way. They were as deep as the car was high. When the car was full of vegetables or other perishable goods, they'd fill these four compartments, two on each end, with ice. I don't know how long the ice would last, but it'd last a good while. It would keep all the goods in there cool enough to keep them fresh 'til the train arrived.

But no matter what you rode, it's the bull you had to

worry about most on the trains. Sometimes they would stop a train and shake it down—that is, make all the hobos get off and march back to the caboose. They'd hold a gun on the hobos and give a signal for the train to move on. So, there you're left. And I've heard, I never have had it happen to me, but I heard that they go down the train while it's moving, and if they run across a hobo, they make him jump off. Some railroad bulls were cruel, and some were fairly decent.

One railroad bull I knew of, he went by the name of Hobo Brown. Almost every railroad dick or bull had a nickname. This one was called Hobo Brown. He was on a division up there north of Charlotte, North Carolina. He would mosey down the track, and if he saw three or four hobos ganged up or waiting for a train, he'd get dressed like a hobo, so the hobos would think he was another hobo. When he got close enough, he would pull out his gun and hold them at bay. He carried a heavy-duty piece of rubber hose, and he'd start beating them with this rubber hose and usually get the police to come out and take them to jail.

Very few hobos know how to guess at the speed of a train. You can look at things along the route and see how fast you're passing them, or just judge it the best you can. But a few hobos—I was one—found out that when you're on a train and you'd like to get off, you can go down the ladder and get in the stirrup. That is the very bottom step on the ladder. Get a good grip on two rungs on the ladder, and when you see a clear place, you can let your foot down and let it touch the ground firmly. If that foot flies up and hits you in the rump, that train is going too fast for you to get off. You can tell a little bit about how your foot goes up to judge the speed of the train. But whenever I would put my foot down and it'd fly up and hit me in the rump, I'd never get off, because I knew it was going too fast. If you got off of one going too fast, you'd really take a nasty spill.

When I would get off of a train that was going pretty fast, I would be on the stirrup. I would swing my feet out in front of me like in a horizontal position, then I would let my feet down and about the time they came in contact with the ground, I'd turn loose of the rung and hit the ground running. You can usually manage to get off of the train like that. But always be sure that you've got a clear place to run, because if you hit a lump of cinders or one of those targets—those little light reflectors—you're going to wind up with a broken leg or something worse. It's always better to get off the train as safe as you can.

I have been on a train a time or two when some hobo for some reason would want off, and the train wasn't going to stop, so he would "cut the air." That throws the whole train into emergency stop. The boxcars have the rubber hoses right below the coupling, and every car has air pressure on it, and the air pressure throws all the brake shoes away from the wheels. And when you cut that air, all the brake shoes go to the wheels, and it puts it in emergency stop. When you cut the air on a train you better be ready to get going, because that makes the whole train crew fighting mad, and no telling what they'll do to you. I never have cut the air on a train, but I was on one or two when someone did. One time I was in a boxcar, and I was lying down, taking it easy. Somebody cut the air on the train, put it in emergency stop. I slid about three feet on the rough floor there and stuck splinters in my rump. It was painful for a while, but I got over it.

You can find out a lot about the trains from the hobo grapevine. That's just a word that hobos use. The grapevine could be in a hobo jungle, or it might be in a boxcar. Usually in the jungle, you can get your information. That was kind of a clearing-house. Maybe there's a dozen hobos there, and some have come from the east, some from the west, some from the north, some from the south. Well, if you're going east and you run into somebody that has just come from that direction, they can give you a lot of valuable information. Where to get off the train when you get to a certain town to keep the bulls from getting you. Whether the local police are hostile or friendly. Where is a good place to get something to eat. We still call it the grapevine. If I'm writing a friend of mine a letter, I might mention somebody else and say that I heard it over the hobo grapevine. It's just a phrase that people used back then, but during the Depression it was a valuable way of getting information.

Out in the hobo jungle they usually have a pot with mulligan stew, and it's understood that if you're coming into the jungle for the first time, you're welcome to help yourself to a bowl of mulligan stew. After that, though, you are expected to contribute something to the pot. It might be vegetables, meat, or maybe you got a loaf of bread or something to drink. Sometimes hobos would want some coffee. Most of the time they would go to a restaurant. They didn't use this instant stuff then. The restaurant had coffee grounds. They'd make one big urn of coffee, and when that was gone, they'd take the grounds out and make another one. You would get some kind waitress or maybe the manager to give you the coffee grounds they'd taken out. I don't know, must have been a couple pounds of it anyway in those big urns. Well, you could take it back to the jungle and make coffee out of it. Make quite a good coffee. There's still enough strength left to make some real good coffee.

But the mulligan stew was usually there at all times of the day and night. Mulligan stew doesn't have a recipe. When you got a pot of mulligan stew on, somebody might come in with some meat that he bought, and maybe somebody had been out and got a few ears of corn out of some good farmer's patch. The old saying is when farmers would plant their corn, they'd put up a sign: "The first three rows is for hobos and the rest mine." On one day there might be more meat in there than there was vegetables, and the next day might be more vegetables than meat. I guess maybe hobos being hungry might be one reason it tasted good. The hobos just worked together and helped one another.

Sick hobos was usually taken care of in the jungle. If one of the hobos was a little bit sick or something, somebody around there usually had an old home remedy or something that they'd try. If the hobo didn't seem to feel better in a day or two, they'd usually take him uptown and try to find a doctor that would treat the sick person for nothing. I mean no charge—there was a lot of doctors back then would. They'd treat the sick person, and if he was seriously ill, they usually made arrangements to get him into a hospital—usually a charity ward. Most hospitals then had a charity ward. Hobos would take care of one another when they got sick. The hobos generally got care when they needed it. Maybe two or three days' rest and a few little home remedies might get him perked up well enough to travel on.

Tumbleweed

Tumbleweed was born in 1908.

I done all of my hoboing west of the Mississippi River. I never had any desire to go back East. I always liked the West—the outdoor spaces. I guess I rode every rail line and branch line in the West and saw a lot of country. I was on the road for about ten years.

Hoboed from 1926 to '36, when I got married. Started on the road when I was seventeen. I didn't really have parents to contend with. My father was living, but there was eight kids at home including myself. I had a stepmother that I thought was real mean to me—which made it real easy for me to leave home and not look back. Now as I look back—as mean as I was, and ornery—I don't know how she kept from killing me. I don't know how she put up with me. She had to be mean. She wasn't mean enough.

Once in a while I would write my dad a penny postcard and let him know where I was. By the time I'd get a letter back at the address I'd given him, I'd already left there and went somewhere else. At one time in the state of Washington, they had the sheriff out there looking for me, trying to locate me. They hadn't heard from me in months and months. And by the time the sheriff got out there to the address they had, I was already back in California. So they still didn't know anything after they got the sheriff.

Back in those days, if I stayed on a job for three months, it was a long time for me. I'd get a little money in my pocket, and my feet would get itchy. I'd hit the road again. I went to California and back seven times on the rails. About each time I'd swing up through Washington, Oregon, back through Idaho and Montana. I done all kinds of work in my life. People sit around and listen to me talk about doing this kind of a job and that kind of a job, and they think I'm the biggest liar in the world, but I'm telling them the truth.

Out in California I cut raisin grapes, and I picked peaches and figs. In Washington I picked apples. In Wyoming I worked in the coal mines. In Oklahoma I worked in the lead and zinc mines. I've worked as a welder. I've worked for farmers. I worked for one farmer in western Kansas farming seventeen thousand acres. That was back in the latter '30s.

I got thrown in jail one time in Los Angeles for "debating railroad tariff"—in other words, stealing rides on trains. Thirty-one days. That was about 1930. I got out of jail and went out to Hollywood. I wanted to see it while I was there. Got a job washing dishes. Then I done a lot of fry cooking. Just anything. If there was any work to do, I'd do it. I drove tractors, combines. Just moved from town to town, from job to job, you know, and I didn't really spend a lot of time hanging around like a lot of the guys did. Some of them, boy, they'd just dig in, stay there, and that was their home. But I'd travel.

I'd stay in the jungles. It was real good, just like pulling up to a rest stop on today's highway for clean restrooms and all the facilities. That was your rest stop. You'd have plenty of water there, and you could wash up, clean up, wash your clothes, hang them up to dry, go somewhere and crawl under a bush and go to sleep and just rest. You could go uptown, leave your bedroll laying there, and nobody would bother it. I'd lay down and sleep with people all around me, and I didn't worry about them. Now, you can't do that today. But I never did stay long anywhere. I just mostly rambled around looking for work.

Everybody was trying to get somewhere. I felt more comfortable being by myself. I saw some beautiful country. I think some of the most beautiful country that I ever saw was up in northern California and Oregon. Washington's another beautiful state. I don't like southern California. I went way down on that Mexican border one time to pick beans, string beans. They had great big old hampers, fifty cents apiece they'd pay for those. You could pick all day long, and damn, if you made thirty cents, you'd be lucky. I didn't even pick a hamper of beans. I left! I saw how slow it was going. I just left my basket setting out there and walked off. I walked down to the railroad track and caught the first train out.

Picking grapes I'd make sixty cents a day. Hard to live on that. I'd cook alongside the railroad track. I'd bum a lot of sandwiches and things from people to eat. Go up and offer to work for something to eat. That's the difference between a hobo and a bum. A hobo will work and a bum won't. He is strictly what his name signifies. That buddy of mine that I went prospecting with—now, he was a bum. He wasn't a hobo. He'd just up and knock on the door and say, "Lady, you got something to give me and my buddy?" He didn't ever offer to work for it.

I'd just think, well, believe I'll go up to Washington or maybe go back to Idaho or somewhere like that, you know. I'd just find out which train went which way, mount me a freight, and go. I was a loner most of the time.

I've been shot at and run off more than once. Used to be a mean bull at Amarillo, Texas, named Ben Brook Bob, and there was a Texas Slim, and there was Green River Slim out at Green River, Wyoming. There used to be some pretty mean ones there at Oklahoma City. I got shot at and run off over there one night in a rainstorm. They was the ones that you'd hear about all up and down the road.

They would just shoot a warning over the top of you, but that was good enough. You didn't know whether they was shooting at you or not. You was on their property, and they was supposed to be protecting it. They was in the right, and you was in the wrong.

Sometimes I would buddy up with some guy, get to talking

to him. He'd say, "Well, where you going? I'm going to California," or "I'm going up to Portland."

I'd buddy along with him until we'd get there, and then he'd go his way and I'd go mine. I never liked to buddy up with anybody, because when I got ready to go, I'd know where I wanted to go, and that's where I wanted to go! He'd want to go somewhere else. Maybe that didn't coincide with what I wanted to do.

One time I picked me up a buddy at Blythe, California, and we decided we was going to go gold prospecting. Back about 1934, '35. We came across the river over into Arizona and went down the river looking for some gold mines back in there that people would work during the winter. In the summer when it was real hot, they wouldn't work them. So we was going in there when nobody else was there. We blew what little money we had to buy staple groceries to take along with us. We had to carry our water in five-gallon cans—be real conservative with it. We'd try to decide what we was going to cook. Well, what one wanted wouldn't suit the other one, and we'd have a big argument. Then it would be the other guy's time to cook. We'd have another argument. It got to where we just argued constantly. I thought before we got out of there that one of us was going to kill the other one.

Well, one night we was sitting around the campfire. I said, "I wish I'd never come on this trip."

My buddy said, "Do you really feel that way?"

I said, "Yes, I do."

He said, "Well, I do too. Let's just pack out of here tomorrow."

Boy, that night we was overjoyed! We just really splurged and cooked us up a big meal and laughed and talked. We was going out of there the next day, and both of us couldn't be happier. We left there and came right down at the bottom by Mexico and went to work for a guy that had a contract cutting posts for a highway improvement job.

Out in this camp, they was trying to teach me Spanish. But

they was teaching me all the wrong stuff on purpose—as a joke. They'd say, "Pass me the biscuits," in what I thought was good Spanish, you know. Well, what they was really saying meant "Give me some asshole."

Once we went over to the house of a Mexican friend of mine. I was having supper there. I'm trying to be real polite, and I'm using my best Spanish—which was wrong, see, but I didn't know it! I thought I was saying, "Pass me the biscuits!"

Man, they got mad! They jumped up and started working me over. They cut my throat. [He points to a fourteen-inch scar and the remainder of his right ear.] Knife hit me here and come down across my throat and split that ear out, and my head was beat in, and my left lung's bleeding, and my liver's stomped loose. All over my arms and legs, there's heel marks where they stomped me. They got me down on that floor and stomped the hell of me.

This Pancho, my Mexican friend, had gone out to the toilet. They jumped me while he was gone. When he got back in there, his own brother was the first one he hit. He jumped in there and got me out—drug me right out of there.

I was in the hospital about two weeks. They didn't think I was going to live, but I fooled them. I hopped a freight and come on down to Lubbock, Texas. I still had bandages around my neck, stitches in my ear. I decided it was about time for me to fold it up.

Like I said, I ended up in Lubbock, Texas. Went to work for a farmer out there and met a little gal that kind of stole my heart away. I married her, but I still had the hoboing in my blood. I had four children, and each one of them was born in a different state. Even after I married, I couldn't stay in one place. I put her through the mill in moving her around, dragging her from place to place, and working different jobs and quitting them. My wife died three years ago. She was an invalid the last ten years. I took care of her.

In 1954, I went to work for the Santa Fe Railroad on a bridge and plank gang. We had eighteen hundred miles of railroad to maintain. So there I was more or less on the road again away from home. Sometimes six to eight weeks at a time, wouldn't even get to see my family. So even in my married life, I was still more or less on the road. My wife went along with it except for the times that I would be gone away from home so long. It was one of the necessary evils of life.

I retired from the railroad in 1973. When I worked there, sometimes I'd see hobos. I'd see them riding the trains, and I'd give anything if I could just get them where I could sit down and talk to them—just visit and find out what was going on out there.

Reefer Charlie

Reefer Charlie was born in 1914. He died in 1994.

Hobos always tried to provide for themselves. They worked whenever they could. If they'd ask for anything, they'd offer to work for it. Instead of out-and-out mooching, they'd say, "If you got a little work around here, I'd be glad to do it if you give me a bowl of bean soup or a sandwich or a meal." Jeff Davis, all-time King of the Hobos—he's been dead for years now and buried over in Cincinnati in the Walden Hills Cemetery—Jeff Davis always said, "Hobos will work, a tramp won't, and a bum can't."

I was a little under fifteen years old on May 25, 1928. That's when I hit it. Things didn't look good for the country then. The following year, October '29, things hit the bottom. I stayed on the road up 'til '38.

I was a hobo. I mean I got a job, I'd work as long as I could, and then I'd have to hit the road again and on to another job. Hobos are migratory workers. A bum is usually somebody that never gets out of his hometown, and he never works. You got a lot of them in every town. Depends on mom, dad, and grandma. And if they have to hustle for themselves, they go down on the street corner, mooch nickels and dimes.

A bum's generally drunk all the time. How in the hell is he going to work when he's sick, nuts, and shaking? They get on the bottle, and they get helpless. Then there's a homeguard. I'm one of them now. I'm not young anymore, and I'm not holding any kind of job, but I'm staying in the same place, so I'm a homeguard.

I was single [and on the road] from '28 to May of '33. Then I got married. I'd just got back from California. I'd been working out there on fruit ranches picking grapes and apricots, plums, apples, and oranges. I came back to Indiana in 1933. As soon as I got back, I went down to the Boys' Club. I was a life member. I'm a charter member of the Boys' Club Federation of America [later the Boys' Clubs of America, then Boys' and Girls' Clubs of America]. I joined it when I was ten years old. I used to box. I started boxing when I was twelve years old, and I had a chance to box in the Olympics in 1932. So I went down to the club there in Terre Haute, and right away they wanted me to get in shape and box that next week. So I was working out for this fight. I was going down to the gym every day, and I bumped into this gal. I must have been about half punch-nuts or something, because I fell into that thing like a chump. And that was the lady I married. It just didn't work out.

I knew I had certain obligations according to law to support her, so I would take off on the road, and I'd be gone a while—a few months or whatever—then I'd eventually come back and go back with her. But things didn't work out, wouldn't work, couldn't work—and I finally took all I could. I was married to her eleven and a half years altogether. I didn't believe in divorce, but I also didn't believe in the condition we had there in the home. I had one child, one girl.

I'll tell you, hoboing is something that you don't never forget. You better not chance it, because it gets in your blood. I can't think of a more peaceful thing than sitting in the door of a nice clean boxcar—a lot of them was clean inside—and watch the countryside go by, especially if it's a nice sunny day. You just sit there and let your feet hang down. It's an absolute peace and freedom. That was the thing that drove all hobos and tramps. Not the bums. I told you they didn't go anyplace as a rule. But hobos and tramps were obsessed with a desire for personal freedom. And peace—peace of mind. And that's what we did have.

Well, except in extremely cold weather. Suddenly we'd get caught in a northern city and couldn't find a job and broke—that was a rough time. You got those people up in New York now what's called bag women and people sleeping in boxes. All of them down the sidewalk and stairways and basements. I never done that. I had certain principles that I adhered to all the time, like Euell Gibbons [1911-1975; naturalist, lecturer, and author of *Stalking the Wild Asparagus* and other books]. He was a friend of mine. I was on the road with him a couple times, and Euell told me, "There are two things that I'll never be: a mission stiff or a sidewalk bum."

That's them guys that went to all these missions where they served free meals. They give you a flop—a place to sleep for the night—and a free bed or free floor space; ain't all of them got beds. Sometimes you have to sleep on the floor. But Euell said over and over, "There are two things I'll never be—a mission stiff or a sidewalk bum." And if you've ever been in any big city, for instance St. Louis, up there by Market and Broadway—that's where the oldest courthouse west of the Mississippi is—you could see dozens of men laying in the stairways. Anyplace they can sit down or lay down, they'd do it. And a few women.

Well, we're talking about from '28—no, '29 was the first time I was in St. Louis. Early in '29 up to '37 or '38. During the Depression years. I even saw women hoboing. One I remember was Nurse Mary. She was a registered nurse. She always carried a clean uniform in her pack and nurse's shoes. She'd get a job in town, get her a room someplace where she could stay while her job lasted. Then she'd get her clean uniform out, and her shoes, and comb her hair, fix it all up, and go right up on that floor and start treating patients. Nurse Mary. I don't know what her last name was. I never did hear of it.

Men didn't bother the women or give them any trouble or anything. A lot of men, of course, are sentimental people, and they thought it was terrible to see women and children on the road. We got it here in that hobo oath that if I meet a boy or a girl on the road, I'll try my best to return them back to their family even if I have to take them home myself.

The oath originated in 1908 when Jeff Davis formed the Hobos of America. Later on he formed Knights of the Road. So we had this code of the road we went by. One part of the code was that you never bothered the women by saying smutty remarks to her or by putting your hands on her. Hands off and keep your thoughts to yourself! Some guys who violated that—if a hobo found out about it down in the jungle—they'd knock about four pounds of skin off him trying to break him of his habits. I wasn't above punching him in the jaw. I had a mother and a sister still living, and I wouldn't want somebody treating them that way. I got it in my pocket, my Knights of the Road card, got the oath on there. The first card I ever held was in '35.

Some of the women, of course, were looking for trouble. Yeah, you found them. You find them everywhere. You find them in churches. I never did actually know of any prostitution on the roads. 'Cause in the first place, didn't think any of those guys had money to spend for anything like that. And if a guy has been riding two to three hundred miles night and day, he wasn't very clean. He's all covered with smoke, soot, dust—sure wasn't a very desirable-looking character.

I remember getting on a train in Montana one time. I saw an empty boxcar, it looked pretty clean, so I jumped in there. When I did, there was two gals sitting in there, young women. It was right at the time of the early '30s when that fad came out and women started wearing white pants and white shirts that looked like men's clothes. Well, they had white pants and white shirts, and they were men's-style clothing. These two gals are sitting right across the car from me.

I said, "How do you do?"

And this big red-headed gal, oh, about twenty-five, twenty-six years old, and a smaller brunette who was probably twenty-one, twenty-two. But this red-headed gal said, "You get back down there at the other end of the car, and you stay down there. Don't you try to bother us, or I'll kill you." And she reached down in her bosom and had a little short-nosed-barrel .32 revolver down there. "See what I mean? I'll kill you."

Whoa! Of course I went down to the other end of the car and sat down there. They went, oh, forty, fifty, sixty miles east. When the train stopped, they got off, and I never saw them again. I don't know where they went. That's the only experience I had like that.

I always had my opinion of that deal. I figured a couple of lesbians maybe. Of course, it's none of my business. But I just thought that by the way they acted. There was quite a bit of homosexuality years and years ago, but not in the context that we look at it today. It wasn't two men getting interested in each other, but some of them old men was homosexually inclined. Instead of a woman, they wanted a young boy. They tried their best to pick up a young boy somewhere. Like Jim Tully [1891-1947; hobo, prizefighter, farmer, and writer of many books during the 1920s, '30s, and '40s] said, "Women are for breeding purposes and young boys are for pleasure." That's the pervert of all authors.

They used to call it a "jocker" and his "punk." This boy would be polite. He wouldn't call himself a punk. Somebody would ask him who he was traveling with, and he'd say, "Well, I'm Bill's boy" or "George's boy." They understood that it was George's *wife*. When I went on the road in the late '20s, it was still prevalent. It just gradually petered out as time went on.

So many of them got hurt, these jockers. I was on a freight one night, me and another guy. This other guy was carrying a little .32 revolver in his pocket for protection, and we heard some kind of noise going on down at the other end of the car. We were lying on a piece of paper sleeping—packing paper that you find in boxcars. My friend turned over and faced me and said, "You just lay still. I'm going to break this up." He went down there—he had a small flashlight—he flipped that flashlight on and there's this kid and this man in the act. So this old boy that was with me, Shortie, whipped that little pistol out, hit the man about six or seven licks in the head, got him up off the floor, and made him jump off the train.

Old Shortie yanked that boy up. He said, "Do you got a family?"

He said, "Yeah."

"Where do you live?" The boy told him. Shortie said, "Me and my buddy are going to take you home, and you better stay home. If I catch you on the road again, I'll knock your brains out, I'll beat your head in."

So we took him home. He lived in Charleston, Illinois. And we took him home and dumped him right at the door. Gave him an order to stay there. There's a song about jockers. It's called "Big Rock Candy Mountain."

I'm a naturalist. My grandfather, my dad's father, was part Indian, and he knew all there is to know about the woods. He started taking me with him when I was three to four years old. He was six foot four, and me about two feet tall. I had an awful time keeping up with him, but I did. He'd see something and stop and explain it to me—what it was, what it was for, how to use it, how to fix it and so forth. This included all kinds of herbs and nuts, anything edible in the woods and in the fields.

If you're broke, you have to mooch it, or you could live off the land—wild artichokes growing along the roads and railroads, cattails by the millions—and there's three or four parts of the cattail that are good eating—and mussels. There's some real good eating when they are fried up nice and brown. Eating them was like eating an inner tube; boy, they're tough, but they have a wonderful taste to them, like fried oysters. I saw guys looking at me and shaking their heads when I'd fry up a bunch of mussels.

Then there was stews if you had everything to fix it with. We had a way of doing that. There'd be two or three of us together, and we go out to get something to make a pot of stew— mulligan stew. Maybe I would be detailed to get the bread, pastry, or whatever, another guy'd get the vegetables, and the other guy'd get the meat. We'd just go to the store and ask the storekeeper if he had anything in there that was starting to go bad. If it were fit to eat, he'd trim it up a little. Most all of them gave it to us or just charged a few cents. I'd always offer to work for them. Sweep the store or something. But they wouldn't let you do it. If you're smart, you'd ask for bacon ends or something that he can't sell. Bacon ends, bacon skins, and stuff like that. There's nothing nicer for a pot of stew, or pot of beans, than a big old piece of bacon skin. Just throw it in there, and it'll season that pot up something fierce. So that's the way we done it. We divided up the duties. If each one of them done what they were supposed to do, we'd go back down to the jungle and have enough to make five pots of stew.

In St. Joe, Missouri, one time, I was getting the meat, and I wanted pork. I never liked beef too good. I wanted pork. And every place I went, every grocery store, they'd give me a hunk of beef big as your head. Most of the time it was about half fat. Tallow. Beef tallow. And that's not good in anything. It messes up your stew. So that day in St. Joe, Missouri, I was on the meat route. I kept on getting these chunks of beef, 'til finally some guy broke down and said he had a good piece of pork. When I got back to the jungle there along the Wabash Railroad, I said, "Hey, any of you guys want to make a pot of stew?"

There must have been about thirty-five to forty guys down along there. About five of them stood up, and I said, "I got the meat here, all you have to do is get the bread, potatoes, and whatever else you want to put in it." So I started to deal out this meat to them.

Boy, in two hours' time there was fifteen fires going down along there. A big can sitting on every one of them, boiling. The stew was just a-fuming up there.

One asked, "Why did you give us all that meat and just keep one little piece?"

The piece I kept only weighed about a pound and a half. I told him a simple answer: "I don't like beef. I walked about four miles to get that pork, and I'm going to eat that dude—me and my buddy—by ourselves!"

Now the vegetables. Well, you bought them if you had money. Most of us had a little money. Occasionally you got it out of somebody's garden. You got a little bunch of vegetables. I never done too much swiping stuff out of gardens and orchards and stuff. I always found that there was a better, simpler way: just go and ask. I went to many a farmhouse and said, "Do you mind if I get a little sack of those apples out there on the ground?"

"No, go ahead and help yourself." And some of them when you asked for apples, they'd say, "Hey, buddy, you're on the road, ain't you? You hungry? Well, come on in the house. I'll have the wife fix you something to eat." And they'd take you right in there. I wouldn't ask. They'd ask me. I have asked, though, when I was really hungry, in desperation. I'd ask Jesus Christ for a handout if I was hungry enough and broke!

There was always lots of music in the jungles. I play the harmonica. Old French harp. I've been in lots of them jam sessions under bridges. That's where we used to have our jam sessions. Some of them guys used to carry their guitars and banjos with them. I saw a guy one time with a saxophone—a number two sax.

A lot of times we met under bridges—bridges and railroad trestles. Preferably a concrete bridge, so if it started raining during the night you wouldn't get wet. Oh, there was jungles out in the open all over the United States, too. But it was nice to have shelter when it looked like rain. You went to bed at night, and you know it ain't going to rain on you. In the wintertime you get under a bridge, on the upwind end of it. You get behind that bridge 'butment, that big cement 'butment that holds the bridge up. You get down there behind that bridge 'butment and build yourself a fire. The winds wouldn't hit you direct, and you can build a fire up and sleep pretty comfortable down there.

Anyway, we'd just get together and play. You'd hear the name of a song, and most of them guys were good enough musicians that if they didn't know it, they'd listen to a few bars, pick up the tune, and join in. I was trying to think of one the other day. "All Around the Water Tank." How'd that go? I wouldn't try to sing it, because I had three strokes in November. They affected my voice. You hear how hoarse? It done something to my voice box. It affected my right hand a little bit. I have a little trouble writing. But this "All Around the Water Tank," it was a nation-wide favorite of all the hobos.

Okay, I will try to sing the tune to you. [In a raspy voice, he begins singing an old song by Jimmie Rodgers, known as the "Singing Brakeman."]

> All around the water tank, waiting for the train.
> A thousand miles away from home just standing in the rain.
> I walked up to a brakeman and gave a line of talk.
> He said, "If you got money, boy, I'll see that you don't walk."
> I haven't got a nickel, not a penny can I show.
> He said, "Get off, you railroad bum," slammed the boxcar door.
> He put me off in Texas, a state I dearly love.
> Wide open spaces all about me and the moon and stars above.
> Nobody seems to want me, my heart is full of pain.
> I'm just a thousand miles away from home
> Just standing in the rain.

You could do that, too, pay off the railroad personnel like that. The brakemen used to come down along there, and they'd usually charge you a dime to ride a hundred miles. You didn't buy no ticket. You give him a dime, and he'd say, "Get on." The division was usually from sixty to a hundred miles long from one division point to another. You could get on if you had a dime or fifteen cents, a quarter, or whatever. You could ride to the next division point. Then when that train pulled into the next big railroad yard, in some town down the line, you had to ante up—give that next brakeman another dime or quarter if you wanted to keep riding on through. A little extra money for him, pocket money. The railroads probably didn't even know he was doing it. Just an old sideline, picking up a few dimes here and there.

The detectives was hired by the railroad to protect the railroad property. [They were called] "cinder bulls" and "yard dicks." The yard dick was the railroad detective that stayed in the railroad yards in the same town. He stayed there all the time. And the cinder bull was the guy that rode the trains.

There were certain railroad [cops] that didn't bother hobos much. Then there was others that were fanatics. Some of them was actually killers. There was an old boy out there in Cheyenne, Wyoming, on the U.P., the Union Pacific. His name was Jeff Carr, and he got killed four years before I went on the road. When I went on the road in '28, every hobo in the country was talking about Jeff Carr. He killed nineteen men there in Cheyenne. He'd either knock them off there with that big hickory club he had, or if they was on top, he'd shoot them off the top of that car. Yeah. He killed nineteen people.

Well, he finally ran into the wrong guy. Those bad ones do. They always run into the wrong one. I got a letter from a friend of mine, Hood River Blackie, died about a year and a half ago in California. Blackie said he was told by guys that knew what they were talking about that Jeff Carr didn't have many bones in his body that wasn't broke. Somebody took a big iron rod and beat him to a pulp. So he tried to kill the wrong man.

Oh, I've seen hobos get hit and knocked off the side of the car. The hobo would be standing on the stirrup holding onto the grab iron—the ladder that goes up the car. The stirrup is that bottom step. And I've seen guys standing on that stirrup—the train running along slow—holding onto the ladder, and a dick knock him off with a blackjack.

I came out of Denver one time in the middle of the afternoon. I hitchhiked fifty miles out to Greeley. When I got to Greeley, I was going to get on this train. There were about fifty guys sitting up on the top. I got up and sat down on the walkway. I had noticed a couple of well-dressed guys, had suits on, shoes all shined up, nice hats on and everything, white shirts and ties. Right away, I knew what they was. That's what they called "jackrollers," a robber, a pickpocket, a thief. They used to ride the trains, and they'd rob the hobos. We started out to Julesburg. I didn't pay any attention to these dudes anymore. Pretty soon I looked back where they had been sitting, and there wasn't anybody there. I asked some other guys, "What happened to those two jackrollers sitting there?"

They said, "They just gone, ain't they?"

When I got into Julesburg, there was deputy sheriffs and town police on both sides of the train. Two lines of cops there. They said, "Come on! Get off of there!"

I got down. Of course, I had a pack on my back like most everybody else did. You carried everything you owned in that pack—your clothes, extra clothes, shaving outfit, sewing outfit, and so on. I got down, and this great big dick, about six foot four, weighed about 275, a great big guy, said, "What you got in that pack?"

I said, "I got my clothes, my shoes, and other stuff that I use on the road."

He said, "Unroll it, I want to see what kind of shoes you got in there." So I unrolled my pack. He said, "Dump it out there on the ground." My bedroll was rolled-up blankets with a piece of canvas over them, so if it rained I wouldn't get my blankets wet. I unrolled this whole thing out there on the ground. He picked up an old pair of slippers that I had in there. They were about wore out, but they still had a lot of miles left in them. He picked them up and said, "That ain't the pair of shoes I'm looking for."

By this time it was dark, and he turned around and started to leave. I said, "Mister, would you do me a favor? Hold that flashlight here a minute just till I can pick that stuff up and put it on the blanket and roll it up?"

He said, "The only thing I'm going to roll up here is your damn head. I'll blow your damn head off." And he pulled a .38 revolver out!

There was a young railroad detective with him. And this young guy said, "Ah, Red, don't do nothing like that. That boy didn't do nothing to you. Why do you want to be like that for?"

The dick said, "Let me get away from here before I shoot his damn head off for fun!" And he went away. I knew I was facing a crazy man! Boy, was he crazy. He was the boss for that division. The boss of all the detectives on that division. It went to his head.

Well, this young guy held the flashlight until I got my pack rolled up. He told me that somebody on that train went back to the caboose and knocked the conductor on the head, robbed him of ninety dollars and a new pair of Douglas shoes. He had just bought these shoes. They took ninety dollars and a new pair of Douglas shoes, and that's who they were looking for, those jackrollers. But these jackrollers weren't stupid. After they done that, they jumped off the first time the train slowed down. Jackrollers done it, and I nearly died because of it. I was dealing with an idiot [the railroad dick]. He was kill crazy. He wanted to kill somebody. He wanted to get me to say something to him so he'd have an excuse to shoot me. I'd say it was probably the closest call I'd ever had with a dick, and I had a lot of them.

Jackrollers lived in hotels, because they were living on somebody else's money. They lived in hotels, they dressed well, ate well. Some ex-hobo wrote a story. "Harvesting the Harvesters" [possibly referring to a 1980s Department of Education series by that name] was the title of it. What it meant was that these regular hobos, genuine hobos, would go up in the grain fields of North Dakota and South Dakota and Kansas working and get a roll of money. They'd maybe have seventy or eighty dollars on them, which was a lot of money for a hobo. They'd start back on the road, and these jackrollers would spot them. They could pick you out if you just came off the job. They figured you had a roll of money on you. They'd follow you, and the first time you got behind a boxcar where nobody would see you, they'd slap you upside the head with a blackjack or something and take all your money. So that's what this man meant by "harvesting the harvesters." The jackrollers was harvesting the harvest hands.

I got a scar under my chin where a jackroller hit me with a brake shoe key. A brake shoe key was a thing that held one of those iron braces on the wheels of an engine. I was coming out of East St. Louis, the Big Four Railroad, the New York Central. We'd just pulled out of the yards, and I got in this car. I saw these two guys all dressed up in there, and right away I knew they was jackrollers. I got over to one side away from them. I didn't want to have nothing to do with them. I got my knife out in my hand where I could get hold of it. I figured if they'd come and bother me, I'm going to put my knife in them.

About that time, an old white-headed man came running alongside the train—the train was going about twelve to fifteen mile an hour. He got hold of the track of the door that goes back and forth on a boxcar. He was trying to climb up on this car. It's hard for a young man to get up in a boxcar even when it's sitting still. This old boy kept hanging on. Finally he lost his balance, and the train's getting faster and faster. He was hanging on the track [of the door] with his hands, but his feet and legs were dragging down on the ground. He was hanging on tight. I went over and squatted down at the door and said, "Hey, dad, give yourself a big shove and get away from there before you get killed. You're going to lose hold there in a minute and go right under this train."

He didn't pay no attention to me. So in desperation, I sat down on the floor of the car, right at the door, and put my left foot against his chest, and I just pushed him. I pushed him just hard enough to cut him clear from the train.

When I got up, this one jackroller said, "What did you kick that old man for?"

I said, "I didn't kick that old man, I pushed him."

He said, "I saw you. I was looking at you. I saw you kick him."

He was arguing, and all of a sudden he had his right hand down by his leg, and here come that hand out through there, and bang, right under the chin. Hit me with that brake shoe key. It lift me about eighteen inches off the floor. When I came down, I realized I was going to get killed if I didn't do something real quick. So I hit him with my left fist, right in the mouth. Knocked him back against the wall of the car right beside the door. I jumped right in on him and hit him in the jaw with my right, as hard as I could hit him, spun him around, and shoved him right out that door. He went out headfirst.

I told this other guy, "Do you want in on it?"

He said, "No."

I said, "Well, then, jump."

He said, "I can't jump. The train's running too fast."

I said, "You better jump, or I'm going to throw you out." So he jumped. I looked back to see if they'd made it all right. Both of them were up and dusting their clothes off looking up my way. I saved the old man's life, and the only one that got hurt in the deal was me. It was dangerous sometimes.

The safest place was in the jungles.

Little Hobo

Little Hobo was born in 1916.

I left home, near as I can figure, about 1929. I hooked up with a carnival artist. His name was Dave Ramsey. For five years Dave took care of me, and in that time we was in every state in the United States. He was a college graduate, he was a musician, he could play most any musical instrument, and he could speak seven or eight languages. He was really a smart man. I think he was the smartest man I ever run into. If it hadn't been for him, I'd have lost my nerve and went home.

I would say he was between fifty and fifty-five years old, and I was—I went three days into the sixth grade of school, so I wasn't quite fourteen. That's where the "Little Hobo" name came in. I was just a little kid. I jumped a freight train on my way home the third day in the sixth grade. I just left home. I didn't have to. My dad was a building contractor, and I could have went to college and could have had anything I wanted. I can't tell you why I did it; I don't know the answer. It was just something that I wanted to do. Even today, I still roam a lot. I've got a truck that is eight years old; and I am seventy-eight. That truck's got 336,000 miles on it.

I caught that first freight in Osceola, Pennsylvania. I went into Altoona and got into a box [boxcar]. It was dark. I knew there was somebody in the box, but I didn't know who. Here it turns out to be Dave. He had been a telegraph operator on Wall Street, and he got a Dear John letter. He had one child. That's when he left, and he hoboed the rest of his life. We went from Osceola to Altoona, and I suppose I might have got out at Pittsburgh and gone home, but he took care of me. He took care of me for five years. I don't know why Dave took to me the way he did. Actually, he told me I should go home, but when I didn't, we got to be pretty good buddies.

The first thing we did after I met him was we went to Cincinnati. We left Pittsburgh and went into Cincinnati. He said, "Buddy, you have to do a back door. You have to show me that you can get along." Do you know, I passed three or four or five of them up. Finally I went to a back door, and there was a young lady come to the door about my own age. I just asked her for a glass of water. You know, I was scared to death; I was only a kid, trying to get my nerve up. What really fixed it was when this girl came to the door about my own age. If it had been an old lady, then I might have asked for something to eat, but I only asked for a glass of water.

Her mother was sitting at the kitchen table, and she said, "Son, you want more than water, don't you?"

I said, "Yes, ma'am, I'm hungry as heck." That lady took me in, and she made me some bologna and a slice of bread and a glass of milk. That was the first meal I ever ate away from home. Now Dave was outside waiting on me. He just was putting me on trial to see if I could do it in case I had to.

He was sure a smart man. At the carnivals he would write "I love you" on a grain of rice. Yeah, and he would engrave your watch or your rings. He had regular instruments, and he did all the engraving by hand. He sold many and many a grain of rice for a nickel back in the thirties at carnivals. Each one said "I love you." He would write the Lord's Prayer on the back side of a postage stamp. He used his own pen. It was an awful lot finer than the pens we use. He sold those. I worked the throwing alleys while he did that. I set up the milk bottles. I couldn't work the rides because it made me sick to watch them.

So my first job was with the carnival. Dave was between carnivals when he hooked up with me. We just could go anyplace and get into a carnival because he was an artist. He never had any equipment other than his writing equipment. We would go into a carnival—or a lot of times we would pass a carnival up. It was really all his doing. For five years we traveled by train from carnival to carnival. He showed me where to ride and how to ride and what to do. Lots of times we'd stay in jungles.

Dave took me once to an alley in Cincinnati to the headquarters of the Hoboes of America. He signed me up. Jeff Davis was the one that started the Hoboes of America around 1902, and he was at the headquarters when I signed up. His name's on my membership card. That was in the thirties. He was at several of the early conventions. He wasn't a very big man, but he was a great leader, a good politician. He's buried in Cincinnati.

My friend Dave was born in the Bronx in New York, and a girl he went to school with married a miner from Spangler, Pennsylvania. Dave and I would stop and see her occasionally. This one time Dave was playing the piano at her house and took a heart attack. Dropped over dead. She buried him in the Spangler cemetery. I was there when it happened, sitting out on the swing on the front porch. He was playing to her in the house. She came out and got me. So from then on, I was on my own. Later on I did a little bit of everything. I've dug ditches, I've been a licensed coal miner, I've got black lung, and I've been a grinder. I've worked all over the country. I always worked all winter. I'd save my money so I could run around all summer. That was after Dave and I split. I've gone back to his grave lots of times. He was like a dad to me.

Now my real dad was good, too—dang good. My dad made me look so small one time it was pathetic. I would come home occasionally. This one time I was home my Dad said, "Fiddle"—he always called me "Fiddle," like Fiddle-foot—he said, "Fiddle, where ya going when you leave here?" I told him I was goin' into Pittsburgh. He said, "Me and mom will take you over to Altoona." Well, when we parted, we shook hands, and Dad left something in my hand. I looked at it, and it was a fifty dollar bill. When I got into Pittsburgh, I got an envelope. I wrote a note and put the fifty dollar bill in it and sent it back.

Well, the next time I went home, he said to me, "Ain't I yer dad?"

And I said, "Sure."

He said, "Ain't you my son?"

And I said, "Yeah."

He said, "Well, how come all the rest of them can take stuff off of me and you can't?" I can't tell you what I said—I can't remember—because he made me feel so dang small. It was pathetic. It was just my pride, but it sure hurt them.

Like I said, I'd go back, occasionally. Once my dad owned a beer joint. He said, "Fiddle, yer gonna stay home and run it."

I said, "I'm not old enough."

He said, "People will never know that. You tend bar for a little bit, and eventually it will be yours. So I tended bar for a while, but then one day I told my dad I was gonna be leaving the first of July.

"Oh, no you're not," he said. "You and I have to go to Evansburg. I'm going to sign this place over to you lock, stock, and barrel."

"I don't want it," I told him. "I'm leaving the first of July."

I left the first day of July, and my dad closed that beer joint. He sent his trucks up, and they took every bottle of beer and whiskey and everything else out. He never run it a minute after. Yep, he never run it a minute after that first day in July.

They always worried about me. There were five boys and a girl in my family. I was the only one that took off. I was in sixth grade when I left and didn't come home to visit 'til I was eighteen. Not because I was scared. More because I was ashamed. I wrote a few letters home, but never once, not once, did I call home. My mom and dad never, never tried to talk me out of being on the road. Never, never. They just said, "You always know you have a home here."

One time I was thumbing out through Iowa. A fella picked me up. I can't tell you the year, but I can tell you Jack Dempsey was a prizefighter—it was back in Dempsey's time. This fella that picked me up was a rough-looking fella, and he was trying to listen to the fight on the radio. I noticed that he had a cauliflower ear. He told me that he was a prizefighter. He said, "Everything I know or done I learned through prizefighting." Well, a little later

I used some rough language, and he said, "I wish you wouldn't swear here, I am a Methodist minister."

He wanted to stop at this beer joint to see if they had the Jack Sparkey fight on the radio. He got a glass of milk and a hamburger, and he asked what I wanted. I said I'd have the same thing. He was telling me that a twelve-year-old boy in his church was an artist and also played the organ. He said, "I'd love for you to hear him." So he took me to his church, and then he put me up for the night.

I had given him my home address. Do you know, he wrote to my mother and told Mom that he'd picked me up and for her not to worry because I was a good boy. Eventually he went to see Mom, and they became pretty good friends. I never seen him after. But Mom would always tell me about him. He was a preacher. His name was W. A. Witenack. Him and Mom corresponded for years.

My mom had a friend named Lizzie Morris. They were friends all their lives. Lizzie was outspoken. She'd tell Mom, "That goddamn kid! He's never home." Once when I'd come home to visit, she asked me, "Do you realize you're causing your mom more tears than all the rest of the outfit put together?"

Well, when my dad died, I came home and took care of my mom. I was in my fifties. Lizzie came up there one day. Mom said, "Well, Lizzie, are you gonna give him hell? I knew, Lizzie, when I needed help, he'd be the one who'd be here."

I'm a precision grinder by trade. I'm a tenths grinder. I grind in one tenth of one thousand, which is twenty-nine times finer than the hair on your head. I ground bearings that went to the moon. That's one reason I could live like I did. I could go to any bearing company when I wanted work and show them a recommendation that I was a tenths grinder and get right on. I could work all winter in a bearing company, save my money, and do as I please all summer.

They called someone like me a gay cat, because I always had money on me. I didn't have to go asking for a lump. Some hobos carried their money in their shoe. I carried my money in the fly of my pants. I'd slit a little bit of the hem out at the very top, roll my money up, and stick it down in that seam. I felt it was safer in my fly. Who'd look for it there? I sometimes had quite a bit of money on me. I've dug ditches, picked fruit, been a brakeman on the Pennsylvania Railroad, a fireman on the Union—that U.S. Steel railroad that ran from Pittsburgh into Erie. But I'd never carry a job over the winter.

It was dangerous on the road. I've been beat up several times. I was traveling with a buddy, and we were thumbing up around Fort Wayne [Indiana]. We were picked up by two fellas, and I don't know why, but they stopped all of sudden and opened the back door. They dragged me out one side of the car and my buddy out the other and beat the livin' shit out of us. I had a broken nose. No reason at all, just beat the hell out of us. Didn't even rob us. It was the worst beating I ever got in my life. And they didn't give us a reason. I was afraid they might kill us.

I did carry a weapon sometimes. Once up in Canada, I had a .25 automatic revolver. I was scared to death, because you're not allowed to have a handgun in Canada. I had it because I was going to Alaska, and I thought I needed some protection. If I'd been picked up with that gun there, I might have gotten five years. I didn't get caught.

I did serve nineteen days in Georgia for not having five dollars in my pocket. Vagrancy. I got off the train in Macon and was walking through town. I was picked up by a cop. I had a little tin suitcase, and I was probably dirty. He asked me if I had five dollars. I didn't, so he put me in jail and on a chain gang. I didn't have to wear leg irons because I wasn't in for nothing serious, but I worked along with plenty of guys that did. The chain gang worked on county roads in those days in the South. Saved the taxpayers money.

I was pretty lucky about not getting hurt. Except one time I stepped off a train going west out of the WJ Yard in Altoona. Some of the fellas that work the yard had a bench that they put right along the track. I stepped off the train at night, in the dark, and expected to go down a couple of feet. Instead I hit that bench. Rolled and hit the journal box. Broke my shoulder. I was skinned up and had a broken shoulder, but I got out of there before anyone saw me and went to a hospital. If I'd been caught, I'd been arrested.

Some times was bad, but some was nice. Like once I got into a boxcar in Oklahoma. I knew there was someone in there. It was dark. Towards morning, I saw it was a young girl. She was about my own age. She told me she'd left home and had been working in a restaurant. She'd wrote home, and her folks thought she was doing all right. She was broke. Her dad died, and she had no way home. She was afraid of thumbing, so she jumped a freight. Her name was Ellen Lay. She was no tramp; she was clean and well-dressed. She was a lot like me—too damn proud to acknowledge she needed help. Well, I told her I'd stay with her, but I'd have to introduce her as my wife, so guys wouldn't be after her. So I just stayed with her to make sure she got home. It didn't cost me any money. I just got her home. She told her brother—his name was Dempsey—what I'd done, that I helped her out. They hid my suitcase so I couldn't leave. I had to stay three days. They were paying me back for helping her out. I've stopped there many, many times to visit.

I was on the road between [the ages of] fourteen and fifty-two. Practically all my life. I never could stick anywhere. My dad called me fiddle-foot. A foot tapping to a fiddle never stops. I often felt lonesome and homesick. But I was so far away from home that homesick didn't really mean nothing.

Cardboard

Cardboard was born in 1922.

I started hoboing about 1937, 1938. The Depression already hit. I went out on the road from Indianapolis. There wasn't no work, hungry all the time. Went back and forth, back and forth. Got work whenever I could. Labor. Picking up around houses, construction jobs. Going out and helping somebody build a fence. Anything at all. I didn't do too much agricultural work. Then I got my seaman papers in 1938. I bummed around Los Angeles. Went out for on-the-spot-jobs. Then hung around skid row most of the time. It's cheap down there. Los Angeles. Get a room for two bits a night back in the '30s. You could get a meal for ten cents in the greasy spoons along Fifth Street. Then I took a freight up to San Francisco. Hung around skid row there. Worked in what we called slave labor markets. Got jobs off the corner.

I've been moving around all my life. Never got married. I didn't want to have any kids and let them suffer, because I used to be an alcoholic. You don't know what being an alcoholic is! I haven't had a drink in sixteen years. Or smoked either. I had to quit. Didn't want to be sick all the time. You get emphysema. You can't breathe. Well, I'm in good shape now. That's from riding these freights, eating sometimes, and sleeping good.

I was on a ship for about three years. A merchant marine, out of Seattle—the Alaska run. Then switched over and went to Australia. I was in Brisbane on a ship. We just loaded and unloaded, and took troops over, and took stuff that they fight with, you know—equipment and things. And then we come back to Seattle. In them days, you often had sealed orders, and you went out so many miles from shore and then opened the orders. That way nobody—saboteurs or spies—would know where you're going. The last ship I was on went to India—Bombay—in '69. But there's a lot of places I haven't been.

I never kept track of anything I did. I bummed around Sacramento. I cut hops there. Working on hop trucks. Picked pears. That was up in Red Rock [probably referring to Red Bluff] in Redding. Then I took a freight back down to Sacramento. Hung around skid row some more. Get a bottle of wine and some beans and crackers and go down to the Sacramento River. Lay there for three or four days and run out of that. Get a couple baskets of peaches and live on them for a day or two. Went down to Fort Worth, Texas—worked there. A handyman. Then I went to Houston. Boy, them cops are mean in Houston. City cops. The railroad dicks, too, but, boy, them city cops!

They had those "P" farms, they called them, out there. If they got you there, boy, they was tough on you. A work farm. Prison labor. You'd go all over the county and work for them, and they'd get paid for it. They do that in California yet. You'd sign on as a county worker, and they paid you thirty-five cents a day or a dollar a day, according to what county. Then they got paid the full salary for a county worker, and they kept it. Those are crooked politicians. Oh, they do that all over. They're all honest 'til they get caught, then they swear it's the first time they ever done anything wrong.

Oh, I done my time in jail. I got put in jail in Charleston for ninety days. They can put you in jail any amount of time they want to. They can put you in jail for a year according to the way the dang judge feels about how much money they can make off you. Whatever they can get by with.

Then I did thirty days in the Urbana jail out in Champaign County. I got on this boxcar in Brooklyn Yard there in East St. Louis, was the New York Central then. I rolled up in this cardboard, and I was back in this corner. It was December, cold as hell. This mission stiff got in there, too. The idiot built a fire right in the door where everybody could see it, and by God, when we pulled up, there was all the railroad officials and cops and railroad dicks waiting there for us. Floodlights all over the place.

They was watching for the fire to come along. They says, "Where's that fire?" Well, this guy, in the meantime, had put cardboard over it and snuffed it out. But the smoke's coming out, and the cop says, "Here it is. Right here." And the cop got him. I was back there in the back. I didn't know anything about it 'til the cop asked him, "What the hell are you doing with fire in there?"

He says, "Well, I didn't start that. That guy back there did."

They wanted to know what guy. "Where the hell is he at?"

"Oh, he's back there underneath that cardboard." He went over to me and says, "What'd you start that fire for?"

I says, "What the hell you talking about? I don't know about no fire." Anyway, I come out, and the cops take us downtown.

They says, "Which one of you guys did start that fire?"

I says to this stiff, "Now listen, buddy, you better not be around me when I get out of this jail."

He says, "He started it."

I says, "No, I didn't start that."

Then I started to take a swing at a cop. I thought, "Wait a minute, don't start that, or you'll be in jail for something worse."

Well, finally, before we got to town, he confesses to the cops that he did it.

The cop says, "Well, why in the hell didn't you say that out there? We probably wouldn't of took this guy. Now we got him in the car, so we got to take him." We went up before this damn kangaroo judge, justice of the peace. Ninety days, man! It was the last of December. I got out in March. When I got out in March, the spring of the year was coming around. They didn't work us, so I just laid in there for ninety days.

Besides that, this guy's got it lousy. Boy, was he lousy. He had seam squirrels from his armpits clear to his toenails. Seam squirrels. Lice. Body lice. Man, he was lousy. Boy, they took him out of there. The guys was going to kill him. They took him upstairs to another place. Then they come down there with a DDT spray gun. Boy, they sprayed everything with it. Seam squirrels, they go around in all the seams of your clothes laying eggs. Then they get on your body and make you itch, and that's where the blood comes from. Then they eat off that. Then they go back down there and nurse them eggs along, and pretty soon you got a whole racetrack full of them. But they're easy to get rid of. You can get down on an anthill. The ants will get in your clothes, and they'll eat all the eggs and the lice, too. But the itch they give you! That's still with you. You got to take a bath and boil your clothes off for a while before that's gone. But that wasn't a big problem for hobos. Most of them ain't got them. A lot of these hippies have got stuff, but I don't travel with nobody no more. I'm a loner.

I been in jail a lot of times in California. Hell, I been in jail in California's Monterey County. I got locked up in Monterey for sixty days there for being drunk. I've done quite a few stretches for riding freights. But I've never been locked up for nothing else. Only that [jumping freights] and being drunk.

You know, back in the early days, I'd see whole families who were traveling around. The Depression. I used to see women on the road. They're bad medicine on the road. They are! They cause a lot of problems. You know what most guys got on their mind. Get in fights over women. I don't want them on the road with me. A woman's place is in the home. I don't want to meet none of them. But today there's a lot of trouble.

It's changed. I've seen changes from old stuff to modern stuff, from steam engines to diesels. And well, it's easier to ride now than it was in the old days. You don't have to worry about railroad bulls much anymore. You worry about these jackrollers— the guys who knock you off for your pack sack. You don't see too much of that around here, but out on the West Coast, you got to watch your step out there. There's still hobos out there—stream-liners [who travel light and fast] and a lot of the oldtimers with a big pack like I got. The oldtimers get by themselves and cook up and stay the hell away from everybody else. It's dangerous now. That's why I stay sober.

The way I do it, I just watch where everybody's at. I don't go around nobody in no town. If somebody comes up to me, I get away. I figure they're scheming or chasing me to steal something or knock me off, so I get the hell away from them. I don't trust nobody and won't let nobody watch my gear 'cause when I come back it wouldn't be there. I get up on the head end of a train or rear end of a train. That way I'm back there by the crew—well, there's no cabooses now, so I get on the head end. But I always travel in the daytime anyway, because when you get in the middle of a train, there'll be a bunch of jackrollers ahead and behind you, and every time the train slows down or stops they all work their way toward you, couple three of them. So I just stay up with the crew. The crew don't bother you much nowadays. They don't care. What the hell can they do about it? They don't care. They don't give a damn. They let the railroad bull take care of you. That's his job. There's a lot of them out west. The best out west.

Here in the east they tell you all kind of lies. The yard workers won't even tell you what time the trains come. Hell, they don't give a damn.

I rent a place across the river in Sacramento now. I used to like to go on a big drunk periodically. Well, I don't drink now, so periodically I get itchy feet, and I want to get the hell out of there, so I know a good place down on the other side of the river. You can get up there and get away—spring water, relax, take it easy. I just get nervous sometimes. I get frustrated. Just listen to all the damn stuff you hear—the crime and the rapes and murders, and they don't do nothing to those birds. I don't even like to read a paper. Don't even have a radio. When I take off, I just sit up there and watch the birds and the things around me. I still do that.

That's why I'm taking care of them chickens over there. I hated to see them cooped up all the time. They're across the tracks there. I found a little wire and everything I needed over there and built them a chicken yard. They was cooped up in a damn coop. Hell, they got so bad they eat two of the pigeons. I don't know who they belong to. The owner hadn't been around for a week. I like animals. I believe that whatever you got you should take care of.

Greenie

Greenie was born in 1918.

They call me a bridger, because I hoboed on the old steam engines and rode diesels, too. I hoboed off and on 'til 1941. I joined the service in 1942, got married in 1949. But the year before I got married, I rode across the western states on diesel. Also made a short little trip in '51 on diesel. I guess that makes me a bridger.

Up 'til '41, I'd travel in the summers and spend the winters in Miami working in hotels. I'd come into Miami and sleep in cardboard boxes in an alley until I'd get a job and be able to pay

$2.50 a week for a room. I'd work as a houseman. I'd carry beds from one room to the other, do maintenance work, count sheets and pillowcases, odd jobs. Didn't always work at the same hotel. Just wherever I could get on. One time in Miami, I got a job in a fish factory where they fillet and process them. They're brought in out of the water, and you are right there cutting off heads and tails. I'll never do that again. When I quit, it took two months to get the smell off me. I never noticed it, but everybody else did. They'd say, "I know where you work!"

I started out from Ithaca, New York. I was on the Lehigh Valley. Went into Elmira, to Williamsport, Jersey Shore, Pennsylvania, down to Lock Haven. It took me quite a while to get out of that town. I must have been in Lock Haven for twenty-six hours. Lock Haven, Pennsylvania. I finally got out of there, went to Altoona, up over Gallitzin Mountain on Horseshoe Curve. They've got to have an engine and a pusher to get up through there. On to Pittsburgh. I couldn't go west and somehow went back to Washington, D.C., took the B&O into East St. Louis, on north into Illinois, crossed the river to Davenport, Moline, up through Waterloo and Cedar Falls, Des Moines, on to Council Bluffs and across the river to Omaha. Omaha up through Denver and through the Moffit Tunnel west.

There were lots of times when I saw big bunches of hobos. Once I got off in Sioux Falls, South Dakota, and I said to this other guy, "Boy, are we the only ones, maybe nobody's working the wheat harvest." By the time the train had stopped, we counted a hundred guys coming down the track. It was the harvest time, and they were coming for work.

I worked the wheat harvest. I'd just ride from place to place looking for work. I ate in Sallies, missions, and in "helping hands." Helping hands would let you wash a few dishes or mop the floor for a meal. And the Sallies, they just give you what you need. I'd go to Catholic priests and maybe get a buck or so. In the Salvation Army in Lasalle, Colorado—that's just south of Greeley—they had prairie chicken. Prairie chicken is like a pheasant or grouse. Hobos could actually get a meal of prairie chicken in Lasalle!

When I worked, I made a buck a day, got three meals and a bunk to sleep in. The bunks were in old buildings like a barn. Oh, geez, there'd probably be anywhere from twenty to fifty of us on the same job. We'd eat right there. Sometimes, if they had a long table, we'd go in the house—in a different room from where the family ate. I'd go from one farm to the next. Through northern Texas clear to Minnesota. I gandy danced, too. Picked tamp and shoveled tamp and drove spikes. Ninety-eight cents an hour in 1940, I believe.

I wore the overall pants, dark shirts, and one pair of coveralls—a full coverall—and a good leather jacket that was lined. I had a small black bag that you could hold up on one finger with a razor and stuff like that.

I never wore a hat. I was catching out on the B&O out of Washington, D.C. I was heading west with an older fella, about twenty years older than myself. He said, "Son, you don't want to ride bareheaded. If you got a bandana, tie four knots, one at each corner, and make it fit tight on your head. You'll never lose it like you might a hat. If you don't, you'll get cinders embedded in your head because you have short hair, and you'll really have a sore scalp." I had two bandanas. I wore one like that the whole time I rode.

I never carried a bedroll. I slept in paper. When you get in an empty boxcar, there would be these long papers like they wrap automobiles or crates with. You could roll up in them. I don't see how these guys do it nowadays with the sleeping bag and all that stuff they carry. I never have carried a bedroll. I slept in paper. Most all the empty boxcars had paper on the floor. If you were cold, you could put one between your shirt and your coat. That breaks the wind, like insulation.

Once I was sleeping in this boxcar rolled up in that paper, about four thicknesses of it—in the far end of a boxcar. I got my spike in the door just in case someone tries to close it. It's about two in the morning, and here comes a thump on the bottom of the boxcar. This guy says, "I know you're back there, so come on out." Naturally I'm not gonna move. I got a little hole where I can see.

He says, "I'm gonna give you another chance. Come on out. I know you're in there."

Well, he didn't know for sure that I was in there, but he took his gun and pointed it right toward the paper. He shined his flashlight over the gun so I could see it. He says, "I'm gonna count to five, and if you don't come out of there, I'm gonna shoot through that paper."

I came out of there. He says, "How would you like to pull ninety days on the 'P' farm?"

I says, "Oh, Lord, I can't do that. I gotta go up and help this fella. I got a job up here, and I got to help him out. He's a poor man." Oh, what a story I gave him. Anyway, he thought he scared me so bad I'd be out of town by tomorrow. But I walked about half a mile—this was a fairly large yard—and I went in another boxcar and slept the rest of the night. If he had caught me again, I know I'd have had it.

Some of the bulls I remember were Tennessee Red, Texas Slim, Denver Bob. Those were bad ones. I think hobos that rode the forty-eight states would know them. I got caught three years in a row in North Platte. Almost got on speaking terms with the bull. They used to ice the reefers in North Platte—put ice in the reefers for the refrigeration. When I went through there, I'd jump off and go right down to the high iron [the main line] where they come back on the track again after icing up, and the bull would catch me sitting there.

In Julesburg, Colorado, there was two large buffalo in a cage, and when you went through Julesburg, you could look out and see those buffalo. There's another thing lots of oldtimers would remember, if they went from Denver to Laramie, Wyoming. You knew if an engine had a 9,000 on it that it was headed up over the mountains and was going into Laramie. All the others weren't large enough to go up the mountains; you knew they were going east or west. Also, I remember in Council Bluffs, Iowa, before you cross into Omaha, they always had a big iron buffalo head on the bridge on the Council Bluffs side. Bet a lot of oldtimers remember that, too.

The fella that told me about wearing the bandana on my head also told me about the shakedown through the desert. He said to always carry water when you cross a desert. That is a must. He explained that if an eastbound and a westbound slowed down and stopped at the same place and there's no water tank, you knew they were gonna shake it down for hobos. Now, if it weren't for this guy, I probably wouldn't have known it. Well, they used to carry these large combines on flatcars. I hopped one, was standing near it on the outside. I saw that two trains were stopping. I knew the railroad bulls were on the train—probably one in the cab and three or four in the crummy—and they were gonna kick everybody off the eastbound and westbound. So I crawled down inside the combine to hide, and I rode on through. The bulls held those guys at gunpoint 'til both trains left, and they were stuck out there in the desert to have to walk out. I don't know whether the rest of them made it or whether they didn't. I couldn't tell you that. At night it gets awful cold out there. Twice that happened while I was crossing the country. They shook them down in the Mojave Desert, but I didn't get caught.

Well, this one year I pulled out of Denver on a DRG&W and went down through Colorado Springs and you go over Raton Pass. There the brakeys would ask the hobos to help out. They stationed all us guys throughout the train and gave us each a stick. In case anything happened to the air and the brakes failed, we were supposed to tighten up the brake on your car using the stick. This was a handbrake with a wheel on top. That was on the Denver, Rio Grande and Western going south out of Colorado Springs over Raton Pass. You put that stick in the wheel and turn it. The grade is so steep going down the other side, it was a safety measure because they didn't want a runaway. I don't know the percentage of that grade, but it is steep. It's the Raton Pass. You go through the yard in Pueblo to Trinidad and drop down into that northern part of New Mexico.

Oh, I stayed in the jungles sometimes, too. They were just places where you could rest. They'd have a steel mirror on a tree where you could shave, hot water, some number 10 cans so you could cook stew and so forth. You could always wash up, hands and face. When you came in, you had something to put in the pot. We'd bum specks—that's fruit with a bad spot in it—or bring something in to add to the stew. Sometimes a butcher shop would give you a few bones with some meat on it. Everybody would kinda pitch in, and the last ones out, as a rule, would clean up and wash the pots, turn them upside down and leave them for the next group. That was kind of a law. 'Bos would stay maybe a day or night, something like that, then move on.

One time a guy in the jungle said he was gonna thump me, beat me up. I pulled a switchblade. I told him to grab it if he wanted to, but he never made a move. Some of the guys had smoke—canned heat, strained. That's Sterno. And some of them would drink bay rum. But for the most part there wasn't much trouble.

We'd panhandle and hit back doors when things got hard. I've hit many a back door, and most people were very nice. They'd give you a sandwich or something, but most of the hobos would ask to do a little work for a sandwich or a handout. They'd split a little wood and so forth. I got smart after a while, I'd ask for a sandwich for myself and my buddy. One lady asked me where my buddy was, and I pointed out the window at this guy that happened to be standing on the street corner. I says, "That's him. He's waiting for me." I'd never seen him before in my life!

You gotta make out. Times were hard—that was back in the '30s. I hate to tell this, but coming through Kansas City, these gals, topless and most of them real young, had signs: twenty-five cents, fifteen cents. You wouldn't believe it. There were hungry people, and times were hard.

I had a close call one night. I was catching on once, and the train was going fairly fast. I had to run, I mean really run, to catch it. I stumbled into one of these low signals, where you throw the switch. It was about belt high. I fell toward the train. Luckily, I just happened to catch the signal, and I hung on. If I hadn't, I think I'd have been under the wheels. That smartened me up. From then on at night, I'd walk up the track at least a hundred yards and then walk back. That way I knew I could run that far with no problem. Didn't take me but one time to figure that out.

I rode everything. Gondolas, grainers, rooftops. I liked reefers, because they were heavier and smoother. I'd ride inside and on the rooftops. There were two ice compartments, one at each end. If the ice compartments were empty, they weren't locked. You could get in, put the door down, and tie a string from the door to your finger. If a brakey [brakeman] lifts the door, it'll wake you up. Then you can get out of there before anybody locks you in. You never know. That could be the end of you.

Another safety precaution was that I wore two belts if I was riding on rooftops. One around my waist and the other through that belt and around the catwalk. That way when I fell asleep at night, I wouldn't fall off. If I fell, I'd be a goner!

And I always jumped the head end of the car. On the head of the car, the rails, the rungs, went clear to the top. There is one on the outside and one on the inside. You could swing up and climb on. If you miss it, it throws you back against the car—or away from the train. Now, what'll happen if you hook the back? You're gonna get thrown right under the wheels! Right under the wheels of the next car.

Riding trains could be dangerous. One guy I know of got a leg cut off. I warned him, but he didn't listen. He was climbing out of a gondola, and when they hit the air, those couplers took up slack. There was a big jolt, and it threw him right over. He was halfway out when it jerked, and he fell between the cars. I was in the back, and he was up front. Well, they had to stop the train. I got off. I didn't want to have anything to do with it. I'd told him, "You better watch out. They're gonna hit the air 'cause we're coming into the yards." He just wouldn't listen.

You learn things. I decided one time when I was coming back from the West Coast that I wasn't gonna walk through Pittsburgh. Normally we wouldn't ride through the yards 'cause we'd get caught. They'd shake the train down or break it up there, so I always jumped off coming into the yard, then walk all the way to the other end to catch out. So I got smart. I grabbed two tankers that were hooked together. They had a platform around them and a rail to hold onto so I could keep running around dodging the bulls. You can duck him that way if you can outrun him. It's hard for him [the bull] to catch up with you doing that.

Well, he saw me anyway and told me to get down. I did, but then I ran back close to the end of the train and laid down, so he couldn't see me. Then I come up between two cars way back near the crummy and jumped back on the same train. When the train got to going real fast, I stuck my head around the corner, and I waved to the railroad bull. I waved to him, and he shot twice! If I'd stayed hid, he'd never known I was on there, 'cause he had told me to get off, and I'd gotten off. But I just couldn't resist it for some reason. He was one mad man. There wasn't a thing he could do. That train was gone. That was in Pittsburgh. 'Course, when I got to McKeesport, I had to get off and walk through, because I knew he'd telephoned ahead, and they'd be waiting for me. If I'd not been so silly, I could have rode on through, across the river and into McKeesport and right on east. It was just something I couldn't resist. I just had to do it. It was like thumbing my nose at him. Like I'd beat him!

Gas Can Paddy

Gas Can Paddy was born in 1917.

Folks wonder how I got this name. I was coming back from California on freights this one time, and I'd caught out of Sparks, Nevada, with a bunch of guys. We got into Evanston, Wyoming. The whole bunch of us got run out of there. Now, I'd been in a little trouble earlier in Evanston and had done a few days in jail there. Well, this old bull that run us off recognized me. He said, "Son, I want you to get out of here. If I see you again, you'll do ninety days on that road gang."

You better believe I went straight to the highway and

spent nearly two days out there trying to get a ride. It was hot and miserable! Finally I seen this old fella come out of a gas station carrying a gas can. He walked a little ways, and I'll be darned if he didn't get picked up right off! I thought about that for a few minutes, and I went into the station and bought me a gas can. When I got back out on the road, two cars passed me and the third one picked me up! The driver asked me where my car was parked. Well, I just told him that I didn't have a car. He looked real puzzled, so I told him the truth. He laughed and carried me into Green River, Wyoming. About eighty-five miles. He dropped me off and wished me good luck. Then right away another car picked me up, and I worked my way all the way back to Cheyenne. After that I fixed up my gas can—cut the top off and hinged it so it was like a little suitcase. I carried a spare pair of pants and a few other items in there. I never had another problem getting a ride from then on! Other fellas began calling me Gas Can Paddy, and the name just stuck.

I was seventeen years old when I left in 1934. At that time I lived in Glenview, Illinois. It's up north of Chicago. I was young. I'd worked two summers for the C-line railroad. But I just couldn't get a steady job around there. I started doing work here and there for two bits an hour, thirty-five cents an hour. Finally I got restless, and I left. Oh, my family didn't like it that I took off. They didn't hear from me for a couple years at a time.

In fact, once I went to a funeral, a wake for an aunt of mine. I just happened to be back through Illinois at the time. I walked into the funeral home in my hometown, and this young girl said, "Hi, Pat, how are you?"

I said, "Oh, I'm okay. Do I know you?"

She looked at me shocked and said, "I'm Alice, your sister."

I could have fallen right through a hole if there'd been one there. I didn't recognize my own sister, because I hadn't seen her for so long.

Nowadays, there's not many of the old hobos left—got some of these young fellas that are still traveling, but east of the

Mississippi you'll very seldom see anybody riding a train, very seldom. They ride these grain cars which, if you notice, got a porch of maybe about two or three feet and it's covered on the top. It's a very safe place to ride. You're sitting there out of the weather a little bit. You'll see quite a few of them riding those. But the trains are too fast today, and they're all diesel.

Now, those old steam engines, it took them a while to build up steam. They get going slow. You had time to get on. Same way coming into the yards—you had time to get off before you got into the yards where you'd get caught. You use to see a dozen, maybe two dozen open boxcars on a train. Sure not many today. Today there's too much thievery. The insurance companies are putting the pressure on the railroads to stop it.

In my day a true hobo never stole anything unless he was more or less starving to death. Then he might find a car with a little food in it. The old reefer cars may have stored a little food— bananas, oranges, and stuff like that, but otherwise they never bothered anything. That train was a hobo's transportation. He knew if he got caught what would happen. But nowadays there's an awful lot of vandalism, and so the railroads keep it pretty well under check.

They had police back in them days too, but you knew to get off before you got to the yards. You knew where the bad bulls were. Some of them weren't too bad, but the majority would treat you pretty rough. Some hobos got beat up bad! I mean really got clubbed bad, shot at. Many fellas were thrown off fast-moving trains at high speed. God only knows what happened to them.

One time this old boy and I were sleeping in the station, in the depot. It was a cold, cold night, so we kept the stove going in the depot. It was back in Glenview, Illinois. When he got up that morning, he packed up his little bag, and he says, "I'm leaving. My train's due through here, and I'm leaving."

I says, "How you gonna get on that thing?" I knew it would be moving too fast.

He says, "You just watch me." Well, that thing come through there, and I don't know how fast it was traveling, but it was moving, I say moving! I wouldn't have dared begin to try it, but do you know, that guy was long gone. He made it! I'd hear many of them guys say they could get on a fast train, but that was the only one that I'd really seen do it. I don't know how he did it or how he survived it. A lot have lost their life trying. I hopped freight trains in and out of the yard while they were moving, but they weren't fast trains.

When I first started hoboing, I went out to Nebraska and ended up in Norfolk, Nebraska. I worked out there for a couple months in a little restaurant washing dishes, pearl diving. I hoboed around Nebraska, up to Minnesota. I did a little of everything. Worked on construction, worked on many a railroad and railroad gangs, worked in restaurants, worked in a few gas stations, in a couple of warehouses, in nurseries. I even helped a guy who was a steeplejack—he'd paint water towers and flagpoles. Worked a while for the state of Illinois, not for very long. Even drove a taxicab, worked for a transport company for a while as a driver, driving tires all over the country. It kept me moving. A little of everything.

But it was Annie finally put the kibosh on it. She worked in a Walgreen's drugstore in Chicago. I used to go in there in the morning. Annie used to cook the best eggs. I wouldn't let anybody cook my eggs but her. Today she won't even fix my breakfast. I fix it myself. But she was a pretty good egg-fixer back when I first met her.

Ramblin' Rudy

Ramblin' Rudy was born about 1911. He was elected National King of the Hobos in 1986.

I rode a lot of fast freights, but I try not to catch a train that's much faster than I can run. They're liable to throw you under the wheels. Oh, I've caught them so fast they'd pull all the

hide off my fingers holding onto the rung. You grab it and hold on
for dear life. You pull yourself up and drop into an empty. Not
everybody'd jump a fast one. In fact, a lot of them just got on in
the railroad yard [while the train is stopped]. It's a lot easier. But
maybe I'd stay in the jungle too long, and the train would start
pulling out, and it'd get up to speed before I'd decide I wanted to
go. By the time I made up my mind, she's moving on. I've always
been a showoff anyhow, and I liked to show these other hobos
there wasn't a train I couldn't catch. I paid for it a few times.

I started hoboing in 1925, up through the Depression
years, right into the middle of it—1925 through 1933. There were
two reasons why I started hoboing: I hated school, and I didn't
want to work. I went to school one day in eighth grade, and I said
to myself, "I'll never set foot in a schoolhouse again as long as I
live." I surely never did.

So I got on old Highway 61 out of Missouri. Stood there on
the highway, and I thought, "Well, if I'm going to hobo, it don't
matter where I go." Here come a car going south. So I just crossed
the road and flagged him down. He said, "How far you going,
Sonny?"

I said, "Mister, it don't matter how far you're going, I'm
going a whole lot farther." He was going to New Orleans. The next
day I got out on Canal Street, twelve hundred miles from home,
broke and hungry. But I knew where I was going. I was going to
California or die.

And I did—from Missouri to California. And after seven
years, I went back home, walked in the back door, and I said,
"Where's Momma at?"

Some old lady looked at me and said, "You must be that
Ramblin' Rudy. Your folks moved two years ago to Shawneetown,
Illinois." So I beat my way to Shawneetown.

I was usually good about keeping in touch. I'd send a
postcard home. I done that regular. Send them a postcard to tell
them I was working, doing fine. I always told them I had a job.
One time I wrote my mother three times in one day. Not because
I was lonely. No, it was a have-to case. I was out in Seattle,

Washington. I was going down a residential district trying to get a quarter here and there, you know. I'd go up to a door, and I'd say, "I'm broke and on the road, and I haven't wrote my mother in two or three months. Could you give me a quarter for a postcard or a tablet?" Three times that day somebody took me in the house, sat me down at the table, and looked over my shoulder while I wrote my mother a letter. All I wanted was a dime or a quarter. I quit that racket! Got tired of writing home.

I hit a back door in Shreveport, Louisiana, once. I remember it was 819 Spring Street. That was a long time ago. Lady's name was Mrs. Mabel Weaver. Told her I was broke and on the road. I'd like to do a little work for a bite to eat. And then she said, "You want to work?" So she got on the phone, and about a half-hour later she said, "I got you a job out at the Shreveport Charity Hospital." I went out there and went to work.

There was one little thing wrong with that job—pushing trays of food from the kitchen up to the main hospital—there was two hundred foot of space that was outside in the open, and every time I pushed those trays of food through there, I'd hear a freight train in the distance. I couldn't take that.

There was a guy that worked there named Delbert. He was washing pots and pans. After about two weeks, I said, "Slim"—I called him Hard Luck Slim. I said, "Let's quit and go to Portland, Maine." I was just talking, you know.

He said, "Okay, but we ought to give them a little notice."

I said, "You tell them now, and we'll leave tomorrow."

So the next day we left and went through Mississippi and then up north, ended up in Portland. We was together two years.

But even he had some habits that I couldn't hardly stand. I'd be in a boxcar at night with about fifty other hobos, and I'd lay down to go to sleep, and he'd sit up and say, "Give me a match. Give me a match." He smoked this Bull Durham. He was always out of matches—and I'm laying there trying to sleep. He shouldn't have been lonesome with all those folks, but I couldn't sleep on account of him wanting matches to light his cigarettes with. He just wanted to talk to me.

Me and Delbert went twenty thousand miles in two years. This one time, we were in Lawrence, Massachusetts, just above Boston, where we'd served fourteen days in jail. We got out one morning, and we decided Massachusetts is too mean to a hobo, so we just walk out of the state of Massachusetts, over to Dover, New Hampshire. There was a fast freight pulling out, going around a curve there. I told my buddy, "You catch the train first, because there never was a train I couldn't catch. I'll get on after you." So he grabbed the train and caught it. Boy, it was moving when I tried! I made three grabs at it, and it threw me down the embankment, skinned me up. My buddy's gone! I'm bleeding all over, and I decided I needed some iodine to put on my wounds.

I went in a drugstore there in Dover, New Hampshire, and put a "B" on the druggist for some iodine. Well, here comes a harness bull—that's a policeman with a uniform on—and took me down to the judge. By that time, I was mad. I said, "Your Honor, I just got out of the penitentiary serving fourteen days for riding a freight train. You can give me ten years if you want, but when I leave your town, I'll be on another freight." I was mad. I was just a young kid.

The old judge looked at me and said, "Well, I'll let you out in the morning."

So the next morning this same harness bull took me up Main Street. It just so happened there was a train going along there. I grabbed it and just waved back at him.

Went on into Portland, Maine. I knew my buddy would be in Portland waiting for our mail. We hadn't had mail from home in about six months, and we expected some. Sure enough, I got to Portland, and he's there at the post office—old Delbert. I called him Hard Luck Slim 'cause he's always having hard luck. We were only separated one night but a long ways from home and were sure glad to see each other. We read our mail three, four times, and went back down to the railroad yard, caught a freight train, and headed north to Canada.

We got under a lot of paper there like you find in boxcars and went to sleep. I woke up in a few hours, and the train's coming to a stop. I looked out the boxcar door, and I seen a custom guard on both sides of the train opening all the doors and checking it down for somebody like us. I told Slim, "We'd better hide under these papers, 'cause they're going to kick us off this train."

So we hid under this wrapping paper. They come to our car and slid the door back. I happened to look down, and I seen old Slim's big toe sticking out from under that paper. I knew these custom guards had us.

They said, "Come out or we'll shoot!" The two guards took us down to the shack, found out we only had twenty cents on us, and they put us on the passenger train and sent us back to Island Pond, Vermont.

I've been deported out of Canada a dozen times, 'cause I didn't care where I was going. When they found out you didn't have no money, they sent you back to the United States. That was back in the Great Depression. They didn't want no homeless Americans up in Canada.

We got picked up dozens of times by the police. Police always said that Slim had a criminal eye, and I had an honest face. So I done all the talking. I said, "When we get picked up, I'll talk us out of it." And I most always did—most always! One time in the penitentiary chow line, he snarled out of the corner of his mouth and said, "You sure talked us out of that one, didn't you?"

I know people got the wrong idea about hobos. But you know, once I was going into New Mexico, and there was about a hundred of us hobos in the boxcar and two women. As soon as that freight train slowed down, every hobo in there took off 'cause they didn't want to get caught in there with a woman. Afraid they'd be picked up for white slavery or something else. White slavery—crossing the state line with a woman. Ninety-five percent of all hobos, oldtimers, was honest and well-mannered and very generous. They were gentlemen—ninety-five percent of them. But anywhere you go you will find one crackpot, weirdo, or screwball. But you can't judge us all by the conduct of a few. Most were good, stuck together.

The jungle was the only home a hobo knew. I remember the first big jungle camp I went into—in Sacramento, California. There'd be about a hundred campfires up and down both sides of the river there. I didn't know much about the jungles in them days. I went up to a jungle fire and picked me up an old rusty tin can, scooped the cobwebs out with my finger, and got me a can of mulligan stew. That's how I started in the jungles. You know, back in the Depression, every town and every big city in the United States had a jungle. The one in St. Louis, Missouri, went ten miles down the Mississippi River.

They even had their own mayor, city council, and everything there. They called it Hooverville. Right in the middle of St. Louis. It was a glorified hobo jungle. Their own mayor, city council, and everything. The farther down the river you got, the worse it got. Up near the bridges, they built shacks out of cardboard and tarpaper. But for good decent people in St. Louis who couldn't pay their rent, there was no better place to go. Oh, the very worst of the Depression! There were Hoovervilles all over the country at the time. That was one of the biggest, in St. Louis. The next biggest was in Sacramento, California.

I can remember everything in detail back in 1928. I landed in L.A. and found Brother Tom in the Midnight Mission, where they let you stay a week—if you can live on onion soup! After a week, if you didn't leave, they'd put you in jail. Well, old Rudy stayed over a week, and they put me in that wagon, carried me off to central station, and give me thirty-one days. Then they let me go, provided I get out of town. All they wanted you to do was keep moving on. So we moved on up the coast. Pretty soon, you learn all these bread lines, soup kitchens, and flophouses. Like in Phoenix, Arizona. That was my favorite place to spend the winter. You go there and stay all winter—live like a king there. You can stay a week at the Volunteers of America, then you had to leave for a few days, go to the compress—cotton compress where they compress cotton—then come back and stay another week. At the cotton compress, you sleep on the bales of cotton. Phoenix, Arizona, was the best place in the United States to spend the winter.

I'll tell you about Phoenix. I had stopped in Tucson, because hobos told me about the restaurant there that feeds all the hobos. I found it. It had a hog trough in the back of the restaurant that went all the way to the ground, and hobos lined up on each side of it. They'd dump the garbage at one end, and hobos grabbed it as it went by. That's hungry people. Well, I thought surely Phoenix is better than Tucson, where they fed all the hobos garbage.

I went into Phoenix, and they did do a whole lot better there. They had a Catholic church. School or Catholic church, one. Every morning about four nuns would come out with three tubs full of oatmeal and set it down. Two other nuns would open an iron gate, and three or four hundred of us hobos would rush in there. We'd eat it with our hands. When you grab a handful of oatmeal and it squeezes out between your fingers, some other hobo would grab it. We was hungry.

You'd go there with your hands black as tar from riding the freights all night long. By the time you got underneath that oatmeal, they was clean as a woman's hands. They fed us that every morning. It was good oatmeal. 1930. That Volunteers of America, they served oatmeal, too, but half the time you'd be wiping worms off the corners of your mouth while you ate it! They couldn't sell it, so they'd serve it to us. Weevils all over it. But that Catholic church fed real good oatmeal, and I ate there lot of mornings. Them were hard times.

I've been hungry. I've been three days without a bite to eat. Two days many, many times. But the third day you get kind of wobbly and weak from hunger. You'd better get something to eat 'cause you get weak. I know one time in Oklahoma I staggered around the sidewalk weak from hunger. Hadn't eaten in three days. Got on an overslow freight out of Little Rock. Like to never got to Oklahoma City. When I finally got there, I went into a restaurant and got something to eat. I told them I'd do a little work for a bite to eat. I was an honest hobo. I always asked for a little work for a bite to eat. And I would work. 'Course, sometimes they'd just let you eat. Give you a handout. They'd give you a sit-down, knee-shaker, handout, or lump.

The best thing you can get when you knock on a back door is a sit-down. That's when you go into the house and eat with the rest of the family, at the family table. You can't get no better than that. And the next best thing to a sit-down is a knee-shaker. A knee-shaker is when you set a plate of food on your knees and try to eat it, keeping the cats and dogs from eating it at the same time— out on the back porch. That's a knee-shaker. And a lump— that's when they hand you something to eat in a sack. They throw you a lump, and you move on. You might get a sit-down, knee-shaker, or lump. The lump's the worst. But the best is a sit-down.

But I worked. Mostly washing dishes, better known as pearl diving. Done that more than anything else. 'Course, I've peeled onions and peeled potatoes.

One thing you find out very early in life, hobo life, is a bakery shop will never turn you down. You go to a bakery shop, and they always had stale or burned bread. They'd always give you something. You could depend on a bakery shop. You could pull into town, you could smell that bakery shop a long way off. You didn't have to ask where it was. You could smell it.

I was down in Miami, Florida, to spend the winter one time. They was picking up all the hobos and putting them in those turpentine camps [work camps for prisoners in which they extracted resin from the terebinth pine to distill turpentine]. We was vagrants and hobos, and they didn't want us in Florida with the millionaires. They wanted to get rid of us. I got scared, but I knew how to get out of Florida.

I went down to the depot in Miami, and there's a passenger train there half filled with fresh strawberries. They move that stuff fast. I knew that in just a few hours that train would be out of the state of Florida. There's some slats across the door, and I broke them off. Went in there and laid down on the strawberries and went to sleep. About three or four hours later, the train stopped. I wanted to know where I was at 'cause I didn't want to get picked up in Georgia 'cause they put you on that Georgia chain gang. I was scared of that, too. Well, it was dark.

I hopped off the train and went across to the lighted railroad yards, and I seen a colored guy coming across the yard. I had my hand in my shirt; I was scratching a bug in there, I guess. When he got about five feet of me, he pulled out a big old .45, and he said, "White boy, take that hand out of your shirt real slow." He's scared to death.

I said, "Hold on a minute! What's the name of this town?"

He's more scared than I was. "D-D-Daytona Beach," he said.

I said, "That's all I wanted to know." I jumped back on that train again. That's the nearest I come to getting shot. I was just innocent-like scratching, you know. He thought I was reaching for a gun. You don't go up to nobody in the dark with your hand in your shirt. Boy, I learned that.

They only knew one thing in Florida. I'm talking about the Great Depression—11-29. That's right—11-29; that's all the judges know. Eleven months and twenty-nine days in the turpentine camp. That's where they take turpentine out of these pine trees. You either pick up turpentine or get put on the road gang. Either one—11-29! That's all the judge knew. Broken record.

In Massachusetts, the law is ten days to two years. I got ten days in the penitentiary and three days in the city jail. In Florida, it was 11-29; in Georgia, two years on a Georgia chain gang. On and on and on and on. Every state had different laws back in the '30s. In Texas, they give you a year chopping cotton in the spring or picking cotton in the fall. There's always these labor camps, and I was scared of labor camps. Tell you the truth, I was plain scared of any labor.

Once in Livingston, Montana, I knocked on the door to ask to work for a little food. There was a five-acre yard around that house, and I worked all day long cutting the weeds and mowing the grass. And do you know what I got? Twenty-five cents and a sack of food to eat.

And down there in Louisiana, them people were hungrier than we were. I hit a farmhouse. That's something you shouldn't do down in Louisiana. The lady had me chop a big pile of wood.

Worked half a day and got blisters on my hands. When I went to get something to eat, she had a sack with a biscuit and a yellow onion in it. A yellow onion and a biscuit. That's all I got. I could do better than that at the Salvation Army.

Well, I just finally quit. Went back home and stayed there just to please my dad. They was glad to see me when I got home. I left at fourteen, and I quit [hoboing] at twenty-one. My dad wanted me to quit hoboing, so he built a lunch stand seven foot wide and eleven foot long. We pulled it up on top of the levee there at Shawneetown, borrowed a box of candy and a case of Coke, and that's how I started in business. To please my dad. And in them days Shawneetown was running over with real good-looking girls. Been in the barbecue business ever since. Fifty-five years. This is my last year, though. I'm going to take it easy from now on.

But if you want to know the truth about it, I have been a hobo ever since I was ten years old, psychologically. At ten years old I was sitting in a room, a schoolroom, and instead of studying my books, I was drawing freight trains on the back of my geography book. My mind was on hoboing all my life. I never did try to get ahead. And I never did either. I'm a pauper. I'm getting too old to travel anymore. Eighty-four years old, you slow down. But I loved life. Happy ending?

The Sidedoor Pullman Kid

The Sidedoor Pullman Kid was born in 1917. He was elected National King of the Hobos in 1994.

I started off in the year 1930 at the age of about thirteen. I had made trips the year previous. I used to go as far as Houston, Texas. Be gone for three, four, five weeks. I was just twelve then. I'd leave on those trips from New Haven, Connecticut. This was actually 1929, a long time ago. I started out riding in the sidedoor pullmans [boxcars], or whatever was available. In those days we used to ride the tops, the blinds, whatever was available. Grain cars in those days did not exist. Grain was carried in boxcars. They used to line the boxcars with this heavy brown paper, and across the doors was a bulkhead of wood. Those were used as grain cars, probably had four or five feet of grain all through the car. They were boxcars used for grain. They didn't have grain cars, not then.

In the old days, we had the old journal boxes where they stored waste. They came along with the waste and a can of this special oil to lubricate the journal axle. So I've seen great changes in all commodities from rolling stock in those days to the present day. I've prided myself, the Sidedoor Pullman Kid, in seeing many changes. Now, that is quite a span. It sure is.

Well, I'll tell you, I didn't predict that I would be on the road all these years. I didn't have the faintest idea, not in the least. I just continued doing what I was doing, that's all. At thirteen, I really became what they call a full-fledged 'bo. And for years I just continued doing what I was doing. Through the four seasons again and again and again.

In the winter I'd go through Texas, Arizona, and California. I played the West Coast more than I went east. California in particular. And I'm still doing it. Still on the road. I do it now more for the spirit of it. When it starts to heat up along about late May and June, I get that rambunctious feeling, and I take off.

All through the month of May, my friends are asking me, "When you gonna take off, Sidedoor?"

I say, "It won't be long now." It's always my pleasure. I have a sister-in-law back there in Glendale, Arizona. She is my secretary as well. She takes care of my mail. I am so happy to have someone reliable. Reliability, such as it is, when I need assistance, is a great thing. I guess Western Union is my friend, too. I wire for some money, some financial capital to survive when I need it. Western Union and my sister-in law are my friends when I'm on the road.

I used to ride the Erie and the Lackawanna back when I

started, the Lehigh Valley. Somewhere, I think in New York State, I got the name of the Sidedoor Pullman Kid, because I have talked about sidedoor Pullmans all of my life. Well, back then you could ride in a box—a sidedoor Pullman—pretty easy. There could be six or seven guys. You could trust them. People were more reliable. You can't do that nowadays. But then you didn't have to be afraid. That was forty, fifty, sixty years ago. We were different then, a species of a different caliber, nothing but the finest people—hobos. We're what they call "class people." We had real class. Today, you got kids on drugs, even in grade school, age twelve, thirteen, fourteen years old. This is a disaster!

Never been beaten up or robbed. So far, so good. It is amazing. I can't figure it out. It must be that my angel is following me around and taking care of me. I was in a place, I think it's Hampton or New Hampton, Iowa—three young punks. They were in a Honda, white one, four-door. I'm going towards the end of town on my way to Mason City. I'm going right up Main Street. I passed the courthouse. They spotted me. This was during the day, almost noon. They said, "Where you going, Pop?" They wanted to give me a ride.

I knew this was trouble. My instinct, my automatic sixth sense, kicked in and says, "Don't get in that car." I figure if I had gotten in that car, these punks would do me in. I follow my instinct. I told them I was going over for a cup of coffee at Hardee's. Later I had a cardboard sign made up, and I was trying to hitchhike to Mason City.

They came up a second time and said, "Pop, we still could take you."

I said, "You get lost, get the hell out of here. I don't want your ride." They turned around and cussed me out. So I got their license number. I put it down, got on the horn, and called the sheriff's office. I said, "I'm getting hassled over here." They sent a deputy sheriff over, and I gave him the license number. I stayed on that corner, and a young couple came along and gave me a ride. I just have learned to trust my instinct. They were safe. My instinct told me they were safe. My instinct has never failed me. My personality has a lot to do with it. Definitely. I try to improve every day. I try to keep a positive attitude. I don't get a big swelled head over things. I keep my attitude in perspective. Yes, I'm blessed with that for some reason or other. I can't explain it myself.

I've done a little bit of everything on the road. A little railroad work, from gandy dancing to—right at the start of the war years—I got lucky and got on as a brakeman for the railroad. The first railroad I worked for was in Niagara Falls—as a switch-man for Hooker Chemical. That was 1940; things were picking up good. War just started over in Europe—Hitler and all that stuff. Things were really firing up in this country. The economy started picking up. We just worked when we could find it and shared what we had.

I'm not gonna knock these younger 'bos completely be-cause they are a good class of people. But the 'bos of today won't share too much of what they have in comparison to my era of hobos. We were more generous and better at giving than they are. Maybe they haven't learned the consequences. Maybe that's why they are so tight with everything they have. They are not too generous. But they suffer some of the same knocks and hard conditions and all that stuff—they have to be survivors, too.

Once I was hitchhiking out of St. Peter, Minnesota, and had just used the bushes to relieve myself. I got through, and I heard a guy say he'd give me a ride. He asked me about myself and listened while I did quite a bit of talking. It was a short ride of about ten or twelve miles. When he was ready to drop me off, he told me he was a sportswriter for *Sports Illustrated*. He said, "I'll try to get you in one of my issues."

I said, "Well, wouldn't that be nice? I sure would be thrilled to see something about the Sidedoor Pullman Kid in *Sports Illustrated*." Sure enough, he wrote it up. I'm carrying it right in my pack. July 18th [1994]. I am a guy that's been around quite a while.

I jumped on a passenger train this one time. I'm coming into Buffalo, New York, from Geneva, New York—the Lehigh Valley. The engineer knew I was on, and he wanted me off.

I said, "You're going too fast for me to jump. Slow down."
He wouldn't slow down, and I had to get off that thing going
between fifteen and twenty miles an hour. Man, I really tumbled,
yeee! I was scratched up, cinders and all. This was in the '30s—
1938, '39, somewheres in there.

I'll tell you my attitude with the bulls: If you want to arrest
me, go ahead and arrest me. I never give them any lip or anything.
And it's worked. I have been so fortunate. I got arrested here and
there, but not really too bad overall.

There was one bad incident. I got arrested on a branch line
that goes into Binghamton through the way of Courtland, New
York, in 1936 or '37. Who pulls me off that freight train? A state
policeman! The train had come through Jamesville, New York,
which is just out of Syracuse. That is where the penitentiary is, the
workhouse, it's called Onondaga Penitentiary. It's a county penitentiary. The state policeman on the highway motioned to the
engineer to stop the train. I'm the only guy in the boxcar. The
highway is right next to the railroad. The cop leaves his car and
comes over to the train and says, "Get off. You're under arrest."

He puts me in the car, and we go to a JP down the road,
and they kangaroo me. They gave me—you talk about a kangaroo—sixty days for just that train ride!

That was a kangaroo job. I served it at the Onondaga
Penitentiary. This was a scam of some kind—this state policeman
and that JP. They [the judges] are working for the county, of course.
They have a quarry there, a rock quarry, and they needed workers.
They are always looking for students to come and help them out!
Each morning they would take all these guys to work, and I'm
telling you there must have been thirty or forty of us in a group.
There would be two guards with rifles, Winchester repeat rifles.
One at the head end of the group and one at the back end. Nobody
was gonna run. You're wearing these big old prison shoes.

In the quarry, we had a wheelbarrow to take the big rock
to the crusher. They loaded it for you, and you had to wheel it to
the crusher. You didn't run with it. I did that for sixty days. What
a stinking thing to do to a poor individual like myself! A young

guy given sixty days just for riding that train. They needed workers, and boy, that place was full. They had three or four hundred prisoners in that Onondaga.

Another thing I remember are flophouses. I just about made them all. Madison Street in Chicago. Boy, that sure was a fleabag. You can get that walking dandruff there in hurry. Those were broken-down, two-bit-a-night flops. Oh, it was terrible!

In those days the way we got rid of that walking dandruff was to go down to the jungle, get that five-gallon gun boat, and boil up your clothes. Make sure you take a good sponge bath, good hot water and soap. That's the only way you can get rid of it.

You learn through every trial and tribulation. The reason why Madison Street, Chicago's skid row, was good in a way, was you got free shipments. They'd ship gandy-dancing steel gangs as far as—well, I got shipped to Essex, Montana, once. They'd ship you by coach passenger train. The coach that they put on that train was strictly for gandy dancers, and they'd hire probably twenty or twenty-five. Those guys got signed up for free shipment. But you better have a couple of cents on you to buy a loaf of bread and some bologna, because that's a long ride from Chicago to, let's say, Essex, Montana. That was on the west slope of the Great Northern Railroad. In those days it was called the Great Northern, not the B&N like it's called now.

I'll tell you, gandy dancing was hard work, and they only paid you, long about 1939 and 1940, about forty or forty-five cents an hour. Board was a dollar a day, you got your sleeping in the coach or boxcars. There was upper and lower [bunks], coal stoves on each end of the car to keep it heated up, and a cook. The cook keeps the wood and the coal in all those cars, and he sweeps them out.

Us gandy dancers worked nine hours laying new steel, all by hand in those days. And you got the free shipment. That was a steel gang. A steel gang was music to my ears—but a tie gang, taking the old ties out and putting in new ties, was bad news. You put them in with tie tongs. You gotta dig out the old tie. They'd lift the track up with jacks so it was easier to pull the tie out. Then you had to clean off the space for the new tie to go in. The new creosote tie. That's a tie gang, and they was bad. Laying steel was a good job. Seventy, eighty men, as much as ninety men on the steel gang—big gangs. You rode in a motor car that had trailers to pull the gandy dancers. We sat sideways on two levels, the top level and the bottom. The foreman, the main foreman, had probably two, three, four straw bosses. They were the ten cent bosses, as we called them. They got about a dime or fifteen cents more than we got. A steel gang is good work.

A thirty-nine-foot rail, big rail. The hundred-and-thirty-one-pound rail in those days wasn't ribbon rail like we have nowadays. A quarter-mile of ribbon rail is welded, and there is no clickety-clackety like in the old days when the wheels went over the thirty-nine-foot lengths. It was clickety, clack, clickety-clack. The faster you go, the quicker the sound picked up. Yeah, I'm talking about the real old time. Good time!

Now, there'd be roughly twenty men on that rail, ten at one end of it and ten on the other—you had rail tongs. They were like a bar with a guy on that side, a guy on this side. If everybody lifts their weight, the old rail alongside the tracks comes out and the new rail goes in. They just knock it over on its side out of the way and the new goes in. That's new steel going in.

Laying the track in the old days, we used a Johnson bar. Heave ho! Heave ho! We had to get in sync with it. The straw boss would keep us in sync. If we made a full payday and had a check coming up, man, we were doing good. But our backs sure paid the price. Yes, it did. Definitely.

Hobo Bob

Hobo Bob was born in 1901. He died in 1990.

I would drift back by my home once every four or five years. In the dark of the night, or sometimes in the daytime, I'd go by the cemetery first. I wanted to see if there was any new graves of my people that had died while I'd been gone. I dreaded to hear it if I got home. So I'd go by the cemetery and look for new graves in our plot, hoping none of them said "Sarah" [his mother]. I was always lucky that none of them died while I was gone. If it was midnight, I didn't care. I went to the cemetery and looked over the fence.

I was seventeen when I started hoboing. That would be 1918. We lived way back in the country in the east part of Tennessee, down in the mountains. It was kind of a lonesome place. I reckon I wanted to get out and see people and see the cities. My daddy said I wanted to see what was on the other side of the mountain. One time when he asked me where I'd been, I told him I'd been looking for the end of the railroad track. "Well," he said, "you didn't have to stay six years. I could of told you you couldn't find that."

Sometimes I was gone longer than that, but I guess I did manage to squeeze in a few months here and there of school until I made it through high school. Then one day I was back up on the mountain, and I met a pretty little girl. I said, "I believe I'll marry her." That was after I'd been on the road for twenty some years. That stopped my hoboing. Well, I did make one trip after that out to Seattle and back, but that pretty-little-girl business kind of slowed me down.

We have seven children. She was a teacher, and she put those children all through college. 'Course, I did help out, but she sent those children through college. One has her doctor's; three of them have their master's. And the wife—I give her credit for all of that. She went to college and got her master's and taught for years.

When I was hoboing, I'd maybe pick strawberries in Texas and work harvests. Way back in the beginning now, before they had all these combines and such, we would harvest wheat up through Kansas as far as we wanted to go. Why, you could just keep going if you wanted to. Then we'd go over the mountains. Fight fire awhile out in Montana and Idaho, forest fires in the mountains. Then we would go on to Seattle and work there awhile. Then into fruit-growing country and small grains. Then later if we wanted to, we'd go on to California and hit the citrus crops down there. Otherwise, maybe cut back through to Colorado, harvest pinto beans or something in New Mexico, and then back to Tennessee. Sometimes a route like that. These years were from '21 into the '30s.

When I first began going west, the Wobblies was still a big deal. But then you could go down the waterfront and work just like a longshoreman. They wasn't strict that way. We could go unload ships or go out someplace and take a load out on some of those little islands. It wasn't near unionized like it is now. I never carried a Red Card [showing membership in the International Workers of the World, or Wobblies]. I never did. Never did bother me at all. I had heard that they did bother some. Some would carry a card just to keep from being bothered.

But we had another little trouble hoboing. We had trouble with some of the railroad men. Some of the crewmen sometimes wanted to get you for fifty cents if you rode. Then they put it in their pockets, and that was the end of that. I had them ask me for the Red Card, but I never did get one. I figured for what I was doing, I didn't particularly need it. I'd just hand them fifty cents or just walk off and leave them. Most of the time I just walked on, paid them no mind, got on the train while they wasn't looking, and went on. All they done was put the money in their pockets.

I have no great complaint about these railroad laws. I never had too much trouble with them, not like a lot of people had. A lot of them had trouble with them all the time. Well, to a certain extent I guess I did. I been put off the trains, and I've had them stop me. Over in the southeast and even in Tennessee, I've gotten thirty days for riding the trains. I got it in Mississippi, and I got it in Tennessee. One time I got it in Texas. You had to watch them people down there. If they got you, they'd give you thirty days. We had to keep an eye out. They'd work you for thirty days on the roads, in fields, and the county drawed it. It wasn't big money then, two dollars and a half or three dollars a day. They draw that like they was hiring somebody. The county took that money, and all we got was nothing. They just worked us for nothing. You could go in and do your thirty days, and they'd draw, say, sixty dollars or something—like they'd hired a man to do it. It paid them. They made that much money on everybody they arrested. And all they was out was what little they fed you. In Mississippi, a few black-eyed peas, and I never liked peas in my life. Breakfast, you got some bacon and syrup.

I never spent much time in the jungles. I was one of these streamliners. I was one of these fast train riders. I didn't fool too much with jungles. I'd get around these depots and catch these fast passenger trains and get there so much quicker. If the passenger train's coming through, you're going to be in Chicago before you think; with a freight train, you're dragging along.

I would go to the jungles if I was waiting over a day for a train or something. I'd go to the jungles, but I never just hung around them. There's a lot of different people there. There are a lot of good folks, but there's a lot of them losers, especially during the Depression. There was some mean ones on the road then— and a bunch a boys. They'd hear of a job, and they'd have money enough to ride maybe a thousand miles to see about getting a job. Then they'd be crying to get back home. They wouldn't know how to ride a train, and if they did, they'd be big-mouthed and hollering and whooping and getting everybody put off by the police. That was the trouble during the Depression. They'd want to fight with you and argue. You don't want your head skinned when you're a thousand miles from home, that's for certain.

I remember hijacking. [Throughout this account, Hobo Bob uses the word *hijacking* rather than *jackrolling* or *robbing*.] We was going out of Montana, and there was four or five of us together. There was one oldtimer, and he was eating the white stuff out of his hand. Back then it was morphine more than anything else. He'd lick that, and he would walk around and around. That night, when dark came, he said to us, "I don't want to be bossy or anything, but I want to ask you boys to lie down in the back of the boxcar tonight." Well, we didn't pay any mind, didn't suppose there was no harm in lying down back there.

The [boxcar] door was open, and later on I saw somebody come down over the side. He hit the floor, another one hit the floor, and old Blackie, the dopehead, he just raised up, and he said, "Boy, step right over there."

We could see through the light. He told the next one, "Now, you step over and stand by him." And five of them came down over the door, and he lined them all up. "Now," he says, "you boys got on this train a-moving, you can get off it a-moving." He had a gun.

Later he told me they was hijacking the harvest boys. Those hijackers would get maybe a few hundred dollars off of four or five boys. 'Course, I don't know if any of our gang had any money with them or not. I know I didn't. When it was over, Blackie began eating his dope again. He just told them. He just raised up and told them. They did what he said. It was dark back in our corner, but there was light up across the door, so we could kind of see. He knew there was going to be trouble. That's why he wanted us to wait in the back.

The next day, we got into Spokane. I saw him that afternoon. He was all dressed up. He says, "I'm happy again. I can get all I want here. I'm happy." He saved us. I've often thought about that. Of course, he'd be dead and gone a long time ago now. I'm eighty-five.

I was going into Knoxville, Tennessee, one time and some fellers told this old man that before the train crosses the bridge, he should jump off so the railroad law wouldn't get him. I told the old man that if the train's going fast, better to let the law get you than it is to kill yourself. He listened to them. I saw one piece of him roll down the hill. The other stayed under the train. I wasn't where I could even go back and see anything else. The train carried me right on across the bridge. I stayed the night [at the next stop] and got the paper. They had it in the paper.

Another time I saw this boy coming out of St. Paul. He was running along and started to catch the train, but when he grabbed hold, it slung him into this switch box—signal box. Hit him in the side. It got him. Killed him. He was just a young guy.

Now at that time of my life, I wouldn't of thought nothing of catching it like that. He was just careless. Didn't look ahead. I saw the same thing happen to a colored boy down in Tennessee. He hit the same way. Didn't kill him, but hit his side pretty bad.

Once we was going right down below Little Rock. I don't remember the name of the little town. I came over from Hot Springs, and instead of catching out of Little Rock, I was catching it down there. This feller walked up to me right before the train run—was a passenger train. He says, "I want you to help my wife get on this train."

I says, "No, I don't have time. I'm going to catch that train myself."

He said, "She's sick. She just had a baby two or three days ago. You gotta help her on." They was going to ride the blinds. We put her on there, and she rode nearly to Texarkana to some little town down there. Rode standing up right there in the blinds. The baby had died. That beat me.

Here's another thing you'll learn on the hobo trail. Always catch the front end of the boxcar. If you're catching the back end, you can get slung right under it. If you catch the front, you'll just get slung against it. A foolish thing I used to do was to get on a car up front near the engine, then run the train. Hop and jump from one car to another, and a lot of times at night. I'd run that thing just as hard as I could. Maybe to get away from the smoke and away from the crew.

Out of Tennessee up to Kentucky, they had all these tunnels—long tunnels. Sometime the train would get in there and have to stop. Man, that old steam engine would fill that tunnel up with fumes. I've had them bad. Had to jump off the train and lay down on the ground to breathe. The fumes rise so I could breathe a little on the ground. Then when the train started moving, I'd jump back on again.

One time in Washington, these boys decided they're going to scare this little colored boy to death about the tunnels so that when we'd go through it he'd nearly faint. They went on and on trying to scare him. He finally reached over and picked up somebody's water jug and opened it and poured it all over one of those guys' head. The colored boy looked at me and laughed. "I'm from Harriman. Harriman! And they can't fool me!" Harriman is down in Tennessee, and he knew all about tunnels. He was more used to them than any of the rest of us.

There were a few colored hobos. Most of them fooled around within a hundred miles from home. They liked to do all this fancy getting off and on the train. I've seen them get off and swing their left leg out in front and lean back and then raise up. I've seen those fellers with their heads almost on the ground before they'd raise up. That's the way that one got hit with a signal box over there in Tennessee. But they was no trouble.

You never knew who'd cause trouble. Mexicans had brought quite a bit of marijuana up through the West from lower California. Then you saw a lot of these canned heaters. Sterno. You saw a lot of guys drinking that, and some of them even ate it with a spoon. I saw one old boy take his shirttail, empty a can of that in it, and strain it. Then he mixed it with water in a Coke bottle and drank it. Down around New Orleans, you could walk along the waterfront and see cans of that stuff high as your head. But the winos were usually just around town, not so much on the road.

I remember an old hobo one time. I was standing in the boxcar door. The train hadn't started. I was young and frisky and feeling good—jolly and happy. The old man came hobbling up to the side of the boxcar. I reached out my hand to welcome him. I says, "Come on, I'll give you a lift."

He looked at me and smiled and shook his head. "No," he says, "I've done and been."

Boy! I thought about that a whole lot. He says, "I've done and been."

That's sure something to think about. That oldtimer couldn't hardly walk, and he didn't have anywhere to go. He just said, "I've done and been." And he went on. Just like what's happening to hoboing. It's kind of done and been.

I hear some of them oldtimers say they hear train whistles, and it really brings back memories. We don't have a train near us now. They took the track out, so I don't hear them blow anymore. But when we go out to a hotel that's near a railroad track, my wife says I raise straight up in bed every time I hear a whistle blow in my sleep. Just that quick. [Snaps his fingers.] You never forget it.

Fry Pan Jack

Fry Pan Jack was born in 1912.

I've hoboed better than fifty-seven years. You're lucky to catch me here. If it wasn't for payday coming up, I wouldn't be in here. I got two checks. I have a Social Security [check] and an army [veteran's check]. I've done four and one-half years in the Second World War. So I get a government [check] from them and one from Social Security. My Social Security check is very small because that last few years, I didn't work too much. Just hoboed. I'm the longest man on the rail but not the oldest in age. Longest time. A lot of guys older in age, but they stay in pretty much. They're not what you call riding the country no more. They just make short trips.

From '28 was pretty good years, still a lot of work. Along the '30s, it started slacking off a little bit. It was still pretty good up until the years of '30, '33. Then it got bad. We had what we called here in Seattle, under Herbert Hoover, Hooverville. We built paper shacks down here on the waterfront and on to the dock of pier 36, 37, 38, now downtown. That was Hooverville. We built paper shacks in there. We even had a mayor in there to run it.

I was too young to really be part of it. I lived here in Seattle, so I was down there quite a bit. See, I come from a family of twelve kids, so I took out on the road when I was young. I wasn't quite fourteen. I traveled quite a bit. In fact, I was gone for nine years. My sister sent me after a loaf of bread. At that time, a day-old bread was about a nickel. I went after the loaf of bread, and nine years later I came home.

Well, you got to remember those are good work days yet, up until '33. Those are pretty good work days. I broke in under good times yet. There were oldtime hobos on the road that shared with each other. You always asked a man for some work for something to eat, so that you could get a little meat or something at the butcher shop. We called him "Mr. Good Butcher." You cleaned up his store in the back end, loading up the boxes and stuff like that, and he'd give you enough groceries for about six people. We shared among ourselves. We'd sit in the jungle and share with each other. We lived good.

But about '48, it got out of hand. Everybody got to stealing from each other and knocking each other on the head to get their groceries. That's going on today. It's not safe out there on that track. The kids have got guns today in the city; you read about it every day in your paper. Young kids got guns.

I was nothing but a fourteen-year-old kid at the time I started. In those days we could climb up on top of the boxcars, you know. And we thought it was fun to run from one car to the other and jump over it like the train men did. The train men had a wheel up on top of the car, and they used that to set the brakes. And we used to run and jump from one car to the other while it was moving. Some would fall down in between, right on them wheels. Run over.

I carried a kid out of Lester, Washington, one time. Thirteen years old. I was working on the section at the time. I was putting the ties in on the rails. We got a call to go down to pick up a kid. It chopped off both his legs. So we had to tie him up and put him on the gas car [a small motor-driven rail-maintenance car] and take him down to town. They had the ambulance waiting. The kid lived. But that's one of those things that happens. You can get in a wreck.

I've been in boxcars that throwed me from one end to the other. It's very dangerous. The car jackknifed. It stopped right now. It's broken a rail or something's ahead of him. He didn't want the engine to run into it and go off altogether, so he just what we call "big fix it." He'd just stop the train. When you do that all of a sudden, them cars will buckle.

The tracks were in pretty bad condition sometimes. The trains go a hundred miles an hour today, or eighty or seventy miles an hour. Well, they went that fast in the '30s, too, in the Middle West, where they're level. If your track is "side-tracked," it's got waves in it. Say that the ties are loose underneath by the joint, and the other end of that rail is packed tight. You got about an inch or two there that the rail can go down and hit that packed one, and that jumps your car, can derail it, throw it off from the track. Now, I've seen a wheel break and drop the axle and cut ties for about five miles before it wrecked.

I have been in three different wrecks—never hurt. I've been throwed from one end to the other. The bad thing about it is a lot of them on the freight trains sit in the boxcar with their feet hanging out in the doorways. That's a no-no. There are brakes on the doors, but that brake can break, and that car—if they stop that thing—that car door can just slam shut. You can get smashed or locked into a car. I had a hand for a little while I didn't like. An old cattle car. Reached up to try to stop [the door]. I don't know why I done it. I spiked it, reached up to try to stop it. It jarred my hand. It took a long time healing there. Pushed the meat back up in the palm, you know. You can get hurt so many ways. You can jump out of a car and get hurt, going too fast. We called it a cinder burn.

In the early days, in the '20s yet, the railroads were burning coal. They used the cinders on the track. So when you jumped out of that car while it was moving, you could take a skid, skin your whole face. Those are cinder burns. That's very dangerous.

Then the railroad dicks. There was about three dicks in the country that I know of that was really bad. Most of them, they were just tough. They didn't want you to break into the cars. But a hobo don't know what's in them boxcars. It had to be somebody working on the railroad to know what's in them boxcars. Couldn't you just see me walking down the railroad carrying a TV? How do we know what's in them cars? It was the railroad personnel [that stole cargo]. Most of it was.

Oh, I've done a couple of times in jail, but never been

beaten. I learned as a kid. They told me it's easier to talk to the man nice, don't sass him. "What can I do for you, officer?" You throw him off guard.

That works, because he'll look at you a second and say, "Oh you're a smart one."

[I'll say,] "No, I just want to know what I can do for you. You having a little trouble down the track, or something wrong, something happen?"

I'm sitting in Gray Falls, Montana, one time, I went to a store and bought me a pound can of coffee. And I was down there in the jungle sitting with four or five guys, and he [the bull] come up and looked down at the coffee. I says, "You want a cup."

"Yeah," he says, "I think I'll try some." He says, "The only thing wrong is the can is too small."

I said, "What do you mean?" He said, "None of you guys went to work last night down here, did you?"

I told him, "No."

It's common for people unloading boxcars or something to come down to the jungle and pick us guys up to help them unload the car. Or load it. [Somebody] unloaded a half-car of Hill & Hill coffee in two-pound cans. Fortunately we only had the one [pound].

We had meat trains what we called reefers [refrigerated cars]. There was nothing but meat on them. Someone'd break into them meats. There's a lot of money involved in that meat in there. And they unloaded a lot of stuff. And whiskey was bad on the railroad. They'd break into a whiskey car.

Now, we don't know what's in them cars. But the railroad crew knows what's in them. Well, you know, we had honor among ourselves.

I'd pack a few little can goods inside my bedroll and roll it up. Nobody knew I had groceries with me. My frying pan was hung on the outside of my bedroll. I had a frying pan fourteen inches. Tin with a long handle. That's how I got my name. I always carried my own frying pan. Nobody used mine. I took care of my own cans and stuff that I'd eat. Oldtime hobo has his own gear that nobody uses because people burn your pans up on you.

If I come into a jungle and find a five-gallon can sitting there with a piece of tin on top of it and a rock sat on it, I'd know that last man left me something to eat in case I didn't have nothing with me. So I'd open it up and look in the can to see what he'd left. He'd leave some beans or a little coffee or something for you. Well, if you used it, your job was to go uptown and try to replace it. When you left, you left the next man something. You left him wood, you left him matches in there and stuff. If you couldn't, that was fine, but you tried your best to leave him something, because you used his. And that's what you called sharing among the hobos. That's the way it was.

You never walked into a man's jungle without being invited. A lot of times they'd be sitting around a fire and a guy just gets off a train. You invite him over for a cup of coffee. If he hangs around too long, you hand him a match. The "rules of the match" was that you handed it to him to go down that track and build his own fire, because you warmed him up and now you want to be alone by yourself. That was his message to go and build his own damn fire. You didn't take him to raise. We had rules. The oldtimers all had rules.

Three Day Whitney. He got his name because he'd come to a town, and if he didn't go to work within three days, he'd pack up and leave. That's where he got his name. When I broke in, you could go to work anywhere in the country. There was plenty of work in all towns. You was allowed to go to back doors and ask people if you could mow their lawns or do some work or chop some wood. A lot of those old girls there would say, "I got a pile of wood out there. Will you cut the wood?" And they'd give you groceries. They'd ask you how many were down there in the jungle, and sometimes give you enough for them too. You always told them five, because before the day's out, there'll be at least five there eating out of your pot. Everybody shares.

You could go to the produce house, work around there, and pick up potatoes and onions. If they ain't got nothing, you'd go to Eddie's Bakery. He'd hand you a broom. You start to sweep.

He'd say, "You swept too much. Put that broom back. Take that box of day-old doughnuts and bread." And then you'd go to the butcher and ask if he got any soup bones. Well, the Depression came along. Nobody had any money, but them hobos were eating good. We're working more than they are. We're not getting that big pay they're getting, but we're getting them long hours, and we are getting board and rooms with it. So that equals up to a lot. You could eat what them people you're working for put on the table. They took pride in cooking for us in the harvest time.

You know what our favorite drink was when I first started on the road? Was Sterno. You know, that canned heat that you cook with? We used to squeeze that and drink it. Cut it with water and drink it. That's a wax, you know. We used to sit down, take our sock, and put [Sterno] in there. Then we'd squeeze the juice out. Then you could cut that as much as you want. But I don't advise nobody to do that because the new Sterno today—it's got junk in it.

And pink lady—lemon extract—pink lady. That was the first drink I ever took in my life. It would make you hungry. Wine would take your appetite away. In the jungle, we'd cook up a five-gallon pot of stew if we was drinking pink lady.

We'd take Bay Horse to sober up. A rubbing alcohol. They're supposed to use that on the horses. We'd cut it and drink it. We just cut it and drink it. We didn't run it through no bread. We just cut it and drink it. Bay Horse. If you see a guy with a bottle of Bay Horse, you know he's ready to go back to work and start traveling. His drunk is over.

We "pitch drunks." Maybe you stay drunk for three weeks, then you wouldn't take a drink for the rest of six months, seven months. The oldtimers, they didn't drink every day; some of them just took a nip every day. I still drink Bay Horse once in a while.

I was never lonely. Look how many people I'd see every day. People at the back doors of the homes I'd work for, other hobos on the road, and the railroad crew guys. I never married. Never married to this day. Oh, there's plenty of good women, but I liked to take off. If they even looked like they wanted to talk about marriage, I'd say, "There's a half-full freight train down there to catch." I wasn't going to get tied up.

We had women hobos. Oh yeah, about the '30s or '32 or '33, babies were born in boxcars. In fact, I was in Clinton, Iowa, one time. I see a bottle of milk on the porch, I ran up and grabbed it. That bull grabbed me. He said, "What do you think you're doing with that milk?"

I said, "I'm going down to the jungle. There's a baby down there ain't got nothing to eat. He's going to starve." He showed me that big walking stick of his.

He says, "There'd better be a baby in that jungle or this thing is going right across that head of yours." When he got down there, there was a baby. He took me back to the house and made me leave the milk. He took me up to the house, and I had to apologize to the woman for stealing the milk. Well, when she found out what it was about, she called her neighbors. They took clothes and everything down there in that jungle for that woman and her baby.

There were kids born in boxcars. In fact, I seen a woman just outside of Denver, Colorado. She's got a birth certificate that reads "Union Pacific Railroad car, Lincoln, Nebraska" and a number on it where she was born. Not in the hospital! She's proud of that. Yeah, her old man was pretty smart. She was already born before the ambulance got down there to the yard, so the old man made them put it down that way. She was born in that boxcar.

It was a family deal in those days. They went to work like harvesters. There were certain districts: St. Paul, Ottawa, St. Cloud. Those are potato harvesting. Planting them seeds. Those families follow certain seasons of work. I followed the railroad. I liked it because I could make enough to live through the wintertime. Most hobos were not broke. Every once in a while you do go broke. Then you had to go to back doors and maybe do a little bumming.

I did if I had to, but I was not a back-door man too much. I was a panhandler. A lot of difference. I'd walk up to you on the street and ask if you got a price of a meal for something to eat.

Back dooring is when you go to the house and rap on the door. I could do better panhandling.

If I go in a restaurant and ask the man for a little work to do for something to eat, I want him to turn me down. If he turned me down, I can stand out in front of his good restaurant and panhandle everybody out there. They heard me ask for work. They'd say, "Well, that boy asked for work. You turned him down. Why? You too cheap to give him a little hotcake or a doughnut or cup of coffee? That ain't enough for that guy. Give him some eggs or sausage or something." They'd say, "We'll pay for it." We knew these tricks.

Today it's very dangerous out on the road. When I talk to kids in schools, or little church groups, I tell them how easy it is for them to get hurt. Now we got "boy-girls." Now a young boy can get hurt just as bad as a girl can. And that's very dangerous. We call those guys Airedales, wolves, Airedales. He's always wanting a young boy instead of a woman. We called them an Airedale. I don't know why they pinned that onto him. They called him an Airedale, and everybody knew what he was. It's been long as the road has been. Because they come to town, and young kids, young boys and stuff, would come down to the jungle. They'd lug them off. That's always been a problem. In fact, I know of good beatings on the road by a railroad bull. He'd come up in the jungle and find an old man with a young boy about fourteen or fifteen years old. He wouldn't say a word—just go over there with that pistol of his and beat his head in. He wouldn't ask whether that was his son or not. He'd just start whipping him. I got in the boxcar one time, I was about fifteen years old. An old man was sitting there. He said, "You're younger than I am, jump out of here."

I said, "What for?"

He said, "I ain't getting my head whipped off on account of you being in my car." So I jumped out.

I never had much problem when I was a kid. You see, I was about 180 pounds. I was a pretty husky young fellow, and I came from a family of twelve and knew how to take care of myself. They left me alone pretty much.

You know, in Britt, Iowa, we have a cemetery where we

got a few hobos buried. Slow Motion Shortie, Mountain Dew, and the Hard Rock Kid was the first ones we put in there.

The Hard Rock Kid [a hobo king]. I was within about one hundred miles from him when he died. I was in Clinton, Iowa, and Hard Rock was around the Burlington area when he died. So the railroad crew picked us up. The bull came down and got me and put me on the train so I could go there. Steamtrain was in the area at the time. Sparky Smith didn't have too far to come. There was three of us that went into that little town of Ogden, Iowa—down there by Iowa City. They had about thirty thousand people that day go to Hard Rock's grave. You ought to see the funeral service they put out. They put us up in a hotel when we came in. They held up the funeral service an hour for me to get in, because I was the farthest one away trying to get there.

And then Mountain Dew died. We shipped him from Minneapolis. He was a veteran. Been on the road since he's been a kid. Centralia, Illinois, he came out of. Little Arthur Parker. He wasn't as big as a pint, but he hoboed all his life. He was a real little hobo. So was Hard Rock. Hard Rock was out of New Jersey. Those guys wasn't big as a pint. Neither one of them weighed one hundred pounds. Some of them guys, they'd be ninety-five, eighty, eighty-five years old and not ninety-eight pounds. And with full beards! Jeff Davis didn't weigh but ninety-eight pounds. Or Scoop Shovel Benson. In fact, Benson and them guys were fifty-year schoolteachers and college professors. Gave up every-thing and come out on the road. Lived another thirty years on the road. Yeah, those guys were schoolteachers and stuff.

Anyway, [during the hobo convention] at nine o'clock in the morning, we assemble at the graveyard. At nine-thirty the Father will come down. Father Brickley. He's the one we got to take charge of the service. American Legion come down, the Veterans of Foreign Wars, and we hold a little service. We talk at the grave, and then we walk around the grave holding our walking sticks over the grave. Then I crack a bottle of whiskey. The first drink I pour on the ground. Then I take a drink. I pass the bottle around to the three or four oldtimers. Then we talk awhile, then I'll give them all a good drink just before we leave. We all drank in the jungles. So we give them a drink. We call that "pissing on a grave." We used to say instead of pouring a little whiskey on the grave of a friend, we ought to just drink the whiskey first, then piss on the grave.

What I want to do is ride a Canadian all the way to New York and then come back from New York down into Britt. I can ride across the Canadian side all the way over. I'll probably do it this year. I wanted to do it last year and something came up. I couldn't make it. That'll be about a two-month trip for me just to get to New York. After I get to New York, I'm one day out of Chicago, and I'm only five hours out of Britt.

It's getting harder to jump in the trains. The boxcar stands up to my eyes. That's the floor in the car. It's hard for me to get up in them anymore. They have to be standing still, and even then I have to have a can to step up in them. We kid each other. "Well, you're getting to that age now you're going to have to get you a little ladder to get in there."

I'll keep hoboing 'til I die. I'll probably die in a boxcar. Or a train wreck. It don't make no difference. It doesn't. I'm single, so what the hell is the difference? They all tell me they'll get a notice one of these days from the railroad that I'm buried underneath a boxcar. So it doesn't bother me a bit.

What's the difference where you're buried? Why go out and dig a hole here or put my ashes on the shelf? Them ashes don't do no good on the shelf. Ashes, ashes—dust to dust, huh? Got to go back into the earth where I belong. Why, ain't nobody going to put no flowers on your grave anyway.

I've thought about where I'll be put. A long time ago I told my nephew about taking charge of that. My body will not be buried. I'll be a-cremated. And my ashes must be throwed on the railroad train, so I'll keep traveling. The jar or whatever, they'll throw it against the train. Broke. A little bit of ashes in each car. Them ashes will stay in the cars, between slats of wood in the floors, and get in the woodwork. I can ride a long, long time. And a little bit in the railroad tracks, too, buried in the rocks so the trains can run over it. And I'll still be able to hear the clicks of the wheels forever.

Gypsy Moon and her King, Songbird (both elected in 1990)

Steamtrain Maury (photo by J. Vawter)

Alabama Hobo

Tumbleweed

Reefer Charlie

Little Hobo

Cardboard

Greenie

Gas Can Paddy

Ramblin' Rudy

The Sidedoor Pullman Kid

Hobo Bob

Fry Pan Jack

The Collinwood Kid relaxes in
a boxcar home

Iowa Blackie: "Hobos never
miss a meal; they just postpone
them."

Snapshot: "A hobo is a complex individual who has broken the mold into which society would force him."

Texas Madman: "I have a home. . . . Granted, the bed may have lumps in it and the roof leaks from time to time, but I wouldn't think of trading this home for any other."

Man-Called-John: "If you ever see a shooting star cross the path of the moon, it becomes a gypsy moon. Every time you see it after that, you want to wander."

Road Hog: "Pray for what you want, but work for what you need."

Frisco Jack puts a Turk's-head knot on a hobo walking stick.

Hobos work together making markers for their departed brothers.

A small gathering of 'bos in Cardboard's jungle behind Gypsy Moon's cabin in southern Indiana.

From the Personal Journals of a Hobo Queen: On the Road

I keep detailed journals of my hobo experiences for two reasons. First, there is the issue of preserving the material. Some experiences demand that I record them. Notice I did not say "write them," but rather "record them." The entries actually "wrote" themselves. They "scrawled" their details across the pages of my life; I have simply entered them into my computer.

Second, writing in my journal encourages me to draw meaning from the events in my life. The hobos taught me to make walking sticks. They believe that a walking stick is symbolic of our life's journey, that any twists or turns in the stick represent the unexpected twists and turns that occur in our lives, and that any scars in the wood remind us that difficulties shape us and give us character. I have spent endless hours whittling and sanding and carving. And I have found that it is in turning and examining and turning and reexamining that I come to discover in even the most common piece of wood a singular and uncommon beauty. The same is true with finding meaning in my life's experiences. The journal accounts prod me to turn and examine some profound life experiences and relationships.

The following is an account from my personal journals of one of my first longer rail rides.

First Impressions

My first impressions of people generally occur quickly and accurately. However, there are exceptions. I had just started noticing the Collinwood Kid at hobo gatherings in 1993, though he had actually been attending various ones since 1989. As I try to remember those first vague encounters with him, I recall that he was strangely innocuous, nearly invisible at times. Though I was remotely aware of him early on, I can't remember having an initial impression of him. After we talked briefly on a few occasions, my perceptions slowly began to form. He seemed shy, reclusive, quiet, very distant, and I figured he must be hanging around the jungle eager to hear some exciting hobo tales to spice up an otherwise mundane life.

That perception held true for some time. Then one fall afternoon, in a jungle in Pennsburg, Pennsylvania, I overheard a conversation between Collinwood, who is in his late thirties, and Road Hog, a seasoned oldtime hobo and railrider. The topic was freight jumping. I was never surprised to hear Road Hog share his wild adventures. I was shocked, however, when suddenly Collinwood chimed in. He told of hopping on trains in high school, getting thrown off trains by the railroad bulls, and—most remarkably—discussing his teenage freight-jumping plans with his mother before hitting the rails during a spring break. She even gave him a note of permission for his first trip!

The surprises continued. The next summer, during a small-town gathering, one of the more daring 'bos suggested that we climb the town's soaring grain elevator late one night. Its ladder was an exterior one, beginning about twelve feet from the ground (to prevent this very sort of nonsense) and precariously rising several hundred feet up the outer expanse of the colossal structure. We challenged several of our jungle buddies. Only one taker! Collinwood was game. And when we discovered that a safety door had been installed at the beginning of the ladder to prevent access, it was Collinwood who nonchalantly went to work with his tools, unbolted the door, and was the first to shimmy up, quickly making his way to the pinnacle.

So much for my accurate first impressions!

Seeds for Adventure

The seeds for a railriding adventure with Collinwood were planted during a convention in Britt. While he was showing me how to read a copy of the railroad freight schedule given to me by Flatcar Frank, Collinwood hinted at the possibility of the two of us jumping freights back and forth between the Collinwood Yard (after which my friend is named) in Cleveland and the Avon Yard in Indianapolis to visit one another.

After the convention, Collinwood advised me (by phone, FAX, and postal service) as I learned to use my newly purchased railroad scanner. During a Wednesday evening phone call, he mentioned having several days off from his job as a nurse in a hospital in Cleveland during the long Labor Day weekend. When I suggested that he ride freights to Indianapolis, he said he would give it some thought and get back to me. I was excited at the prospect. I had recorded the stories of hobos and their lives on the road both on my computer and in my heart for more than a decade; yet their road would remain for me an enigma never to be fully understood without walking the proverbial mile in their shoes. I had taken numerous short one- or two-day trips, but a week-long experience would be an insightful beginning.

The next call came Friday afternoon. "What are you doing for the next five days?" he asked. I could hear the railroad scanner in the background as he spoke.

As we considered our plans, Collinwood was going down his computerized railriding check list. I could picture him methodically placing each item in a laundry basket in preparation for arranging it all in his backpack. "I plan to pack up and head for the Collinwood yards. If I'm lucky enough to catch out on the BUIN (Buffalo to Indianapolis) tonight, I could be in Indy by morning," he speculated.

I looked at my watch. It was 5:30 P.M. Indianapolis time, 6:30 P.M. Cleveland time. I had practically memorized from my freight schedule all the trains passing through both Cleveland and the Indianapolis Avon yards. "Collinwood, the BUIN was due in Cleveland over an hour ago. You'll never make it!" He calmly explained that trains are rarely on time, that he had heard it arrive at 10:00 P.M. the previous night, that nothing on the scanner indicated that it had yet arrived tonight, and, finally, if he missed it—he simply missed it.

I thought for a moment before responding. "I'll assume if I haven't heard from you by eleven tonight that you caught the train, and I'll be in the Avon yards at 5:30 in the morning to pick you up." (I'd also memorized arrival times.)

"Don't assume anything," he ordered. "Train hopping's far too unpredictable. Just stay put, and I'll call you when and if I make it. You can come to the yards then and pick me up. We'll go back to your cabin in Nashville, check your gear, and decide what to do from there." As I hung up, I couldn't understand why he would have so many doubts. After all, the schedule was printed out clearly in my freight schedule book.

My backpack is always loaded and hanging on my door, not anticipating railriding, but ready for a hike-in-a-heartbeat whenever the Brown County hills beckon me. I quickly adapted it to my needs on the tracks and settled in for what would be my last good night's rest for several days. Before turning out my bedside light that evening, I couldn't resist dialing Collinwood's house. The message had been changed: "I'm not here right now. I don't know where I am, and I don't know when I'll be back. Please leave a message after the beep, and I might get back to you."

I didn't set the alarm; I was certain Collinwood's morning call would wake me. When I awoke and saw the clock reading 7:55 A.M., I reached for the phone to check for a dial tone. It was not out of order. I had made arrangements to leave my dog Moon Shadow at a local kennel that would close promptly at noon. As 11:00 A.M. rolled by, I struggled with a decision. Should I leave the phone for the fifteen minutes it would take to speed to the Bean

Blossom Kennel before it closed, or stick by the phone and risk having to make other provisions for Shadow? It was a holiday weekend, and most kennels (all kennels?) were probably booked full. I would await Collinwood's call.

I resisted thinking about what trouble had detained him. I am generally optimistic, but I was being challenged. Keeping my mind busy, I did laundry, cleaned the fridge, and diced fresh peaches, which I knew would not keep until I returned.

At 11:20 A.M. the phone rang. It was Collinwood. In the most composed voice I could muster, I asked, "Where are you?"

"Do you really want to know?" he answered. It's not very assuring when someone answers a question with another question.

I asked again without the composure, "Where are you, Collinwood?"

A faint chuckle on the other end. "I'm in Indy at the Avon Yard."

Preparations

Less than an hour and a half later, I pulled up behind the Burger King near the yard. There sat Collinwood on a patch of grass between fast-food parking and a small strip mall. He was making notes on three-by-five cards. We retrieved his pack, which he had hidden beside a daycare center, and we spent the next hour driving every possible road, lane, and path that led to the yards, attempting to gather valuable information so we could catch out after dark.

On the drive to Brown County, Collinwood began sharing, from note cards, the carefully recorded details of his trip from Cleveland. I had become accustomed to and fascinated by his long, vivid, epic accounts and explanations, so I hardly noticed how much time had elapsed when he concluded his story a couple of hours later sitting on my couch and eating a bowl of fresh peaches and ice cream. How strange, I thought, that I once considered him quiet.

I gave him a quick tour of my property—the jungle and bunkhouse—before we began the task of comparing the contents of my pack against his checklist and making the appropriate additions. I needed boots with better ankle support, Chapstick (Collinwood had sunscreen), and a knit cap or scarf. I had only forty dollars in cash and one credit card. Collinwood, on the other hand, had stashed two hundred dollars in the sole of each boot and two hundred more in his wallet along with several major credit cards! He explained that he always wanted enough cash to post his bail should he be apprehended. It was about 5:00 P.M. when we headed back toward Indianapolis. Collinwood was adamant about two points: I had to have earphones for my new scanner; he had to have a veggies and cheese Subway sandwich for the road. We made both stops on the way to the yard.

Collinwood directed me down a few of the previously explored back roads before deciding on just the right spot to hide our gear. Then we drove to the strip mall to park my car, with a prayer that it would still be there when we returned. I carefully placed a note under the wiper blade: WILL PICK TRUCK UP LATER. MECHANICAL TROUBLE. Walking back through the darkness to our hiding place, we listened carefully to our scanners and considered several questions: Which direction do we want to go? Should we decide on a firm destination, or are we comfortable just allowing the road to carry us along? We both agreed that we preferred to head east, but that we were far more interested in adventure than destination.

Rolling Nowhere

Finally, we came to our packs, heaved them onto our backs, and stood quietly. In that short, dark silence, I pondered my sanity. I had little experience jumping freights out of yards on long rides. Most of my train hopping had been spontaneous, short rides out from grain elevators—generally with the crews' secret knowledge and blessing. Here we stood alongside the Avon Yard. It was large and active. Trucks and crews hustled about at this dark hour busily attending to their respective responsibilities. Trains moved in and out steadily from the hump yard, where there was startling activity as one consist after another was disassembled and reassembled. High-security cars came and left regularly on various trains, and a healthy staff of railroad police were taking their jobs seriously, buzzing about with high-beam spotlights.

I paused, pressed under the weight of my pack and the weight of a decision. It wasn't too late to change my mind. I was surprised at how easily I resigned myself to a rare attitude of subordination and dependence. I would watch Collinwood closely, take his lead, and not question his judgment. I focused my attention on his face, and for the first time I watched his remarkable process of problem-solving, which I would soon come to perceive as both brilliant and reassuring. It would begin simply with a facial expression—one that reflected not worry, but an eagerness to accept a challenge.

Then came the discourse—a stream-of-consciousness monologue: "In front of us are the fuel tanks. No one there right now. The receiving yards are beyond our view. Ahead and to the left, I see several trains made up and, more than likely, going east eventually. We have a few questions: Can we get to them without being spotted? Yes, I think so, if we can quickly get in between any two trains and stay in the shadows. Where are those trains headed? Don't know that yet, because there's been no information on the scanner. It really isn't that important, though, since we've already decided that we aren't so concerned with destination. When do those trains leave? That information hasn't been announced on the scanner yet, but my best guess is that the one with the freddy on the back is pretty close to rolling out. So we have a number of options, but I think our best bet is the train with the freddy."

I looked at the freddy, the computerized flashing rear-end device which has replaced the former function of a brakeman in the caboose in transmitting information to the crew. Then Collinwood looked at me for the first time in the thought process. "Look over to your right. This afternoon I noticed a portion of fence and a concrete post down across the drainage ditch. We can cross over there. Follow me."

Once we began moving, the pace was fast and constant. Over the fence, across four or five tracks, and presto! we were in the shadows and between two waiting trains with no engines. The jumble on the scanner gave no indication that we'd been spotted. Collinwood moved swiftly; I was on his heels. "We're just looking for a ride right now," he said, "any possible ride. We can find one, then improve on it while we wait." We continued hurriedly, the ballast crunching under our boots. "Look," he shouted in a whisper, "a grain car with a porch! It's easy to be seen on one, but the risk is less at night. Count the cars now, so we can find our way back if we don't find anything better." Counting seemed to slow me down. I looked up and saw that Collinwood was several paces ahead. He stopped suddenly and veered to the left. "We're home," he smiled, as he peered into the open doors of a huge, double-long boxcar.

He flashed a beam from his little flashlight onto the floor, rubbed a couple fingers over the surface, and inspected the residue. "Sometimes there's a chemical deposit left in a car. You always want to pass those up. This one looks a little greasy but no chemicals." We lifted our gear into it and continued walking a short distance.

He scrambled up into a couple of gondolas, open-top cars with high sides, searching for pieces of two-by-fours or railroad spikes to secure the boxcar doors; I checked along the ground. When we'd found three pieces, I climbed aboard our car (a less than graceful feat for someone five feet three inches tall) and offered Collinwood my hand. Once in the car, he used a chunk of steel from the tracks to hammer in the two-by-fours to prevent the doors from shifting. Then it occurred to him that because this double-long box had two doors on each side, movement that would shift one door closed would shift the other door open, so in this case there was no danger that the doors would lock shut. He decided to take the precaution anyway to prevent any movement during our trip.

Before long Collinwood reported, "Scanner says this

train's headed to Elkhart. If that's all right with you, it's all right with me. I know the Elkhart Yard well, and we can get anywhere from Elkhart."

We heard the air in the brakes. Collinwood said with a grin, "Count to ten and hang on!" Sure enough, the train gave a jerk and began to groan out of the yard. We stayed hidden in the corner until we were out of sight. Collinwood grabbed a strap (similar to a heavy nylon dog leash) and ran it through a metal opening beside the door, knotted it securely, and tied it into a loop at the loose end. He called it a boxcar strap and directed me to hold onto it when I stood near the door to look out. We rolled past the airport, the Eli Lilly facility, Fountain Square, the Old East Side, and slowly away from the big city lights.

Prime Time

In the rural darkness, we were securely hidden from sight. We positioned our cardboard and foam pads on the floor across from the huge twenty-foot-wide door opening and sat down. Collinwood stretched his arms out dramatically toward the rectangular hole before us. "Our large-screen TV," he announced.

And what a program! The pitch-dark sky was studded with stars. And in the upper left-hand corner, an amazing three-quarter moon threw a massive shaft of light diagonally across the floor, bathing us in lunar magic. An occasional blur would flash across our screen: a blinking railroad crossing, a small town, a barnyard aglow with tractor lights. We sat silently for a long time studying our screen. Prime time.

Collinwood had been on the road now for more than twenty-four hours. He glanced my way and warned, "I don't think we should sit here much longer." I looked puzzled. "Moonburn," he laughed heartily. "I brought sunscreen, but forgot my moonscreen!"

As he prepared to bed down, he first stretched out a layer of thick black plastic, then a couple layers of cardboard, and finally his bedroll. A few items of clothing in a small cloth bag would serve as his pillow. As I was arranging my foam rubber pad on the black plastic with my bedroll on top, Collinwood said, "I always sleep on my bedroll, but I bring this along for fun." He had pulled a hammock from his pack and was stringing it up in the boxcar. "You can't go railriding without trying this." He held it open as I climbed in for a few short but enjoyable moments.

Half an hour later, we were bedded down in our sleeping bags for the night. Collinwood's bedroll was a few feet from mine, but we still had to scream to talk over the noise of the fast-moving train. After a few minutes, Collinwood began to climb out of his roll. Barefoot and in his long johns, he stumbled around and behind me toward the boxcar door. "Gotta pee," he apologized. "Hope you don't mind my long johns." I couldn't help thinking that life isn't always fair. Peeing out the boxcar door was not an option for me. I would wait until morning.

Within minutes of returning to his bedroll, Collinwood fell asleep in the middle of a sentence. Sleep would not come as easily for me. I finally crawled out of my bag, slipped my boots on loosely, and went back to sit on the one small scrap of cardboard that we'd left in front of the door.

It was different watching the night sky by myself. In an eerie way, I felt as though the stars were watching me. It seemed possible that they could suck me mysteriously out the door and into the Milky Way—and even more possible that I would not resist. Rolling through star-studded Hoosier farmland on a freight train, I felt—as never before—the satisfaction and wholeness that comes from being a small yet integral part of something vast and complete. It was an uncommon moment of awareness. I thought for a second about waking Collinwood, but I questioned whether such enchantment could be shared.

An hour later, I was back in my sleeping bag and marveling at Collinwood's ability to rest. I could faintly see the silhouette of his head bobbing in rhythm with the train. As I drifted sporadically off to sleep, I was reliving the day's experience—and pondering first impressions. Somewhere in the night, I was aware that our train had stopped. The stillness and quiet, which I welcomed but did not understand, finally allowed a sound sleep.

I heard Collinwood step over me, and I squinted at the morning sun streaming into our car. I turned away to offer him privacy at the door. He was mumbling something about a cemetery. "We've been here for several hours," I told him as I tugged curiously at my sleeping bag, noticing that the zipper which had been on my right last night was now twisted entirely around on my left. Concerned that our train had dropped off a section of cars, including ours, and gone on without us, I asked, "Do you suppose we've been set off ?"

"Can't say for sure," he answered as he crawled back into his roll, "but I do know this: I don't want to deal with it right now." Astoundingly, within seconds he was asleep again. I climbed out of my sleeping bag, stepped directly into my boots, and staggered to the door.

The scene was remarkable. Within fifty feet of our train was a massive old cemetery stretching as far as I could see in every direction. Beautiful mature trees were interspersed among a field of ancient markers, and the warm morning sun meeting the cool grasses had created small ground clouds which settled gracefully here and there. I sat down on the ragged piece of cardboard again and gazed out the door with the same wonder as I had during the night. Same screen; different scene. Our program continued to unfold.

Marion to Elkhart

It was more than an hour before Collinwood awoke. "Well," he said calmly, "I'd like to think we're in Elkhart, but I think we've been set off quite a distance away. I'll go for a walk and try to figure it out." He returned about twenty minutes later carrying a paper bag. "We're in Marion, Indiana," he explained. "Let's pack up our gear and go to the cemetery for breakfast." I slipped down out of the car, over a thick accumulation of grease. Collinwood shook his head at the black oily grime streaking the back of my jeans.

I spread out plastic and a bedroll on the grass, and Collinwood unpacked breakfast: sweet rolls, chocolate malt ice cream, and soda! I looked at our section of dead cars. "What happened?" I asked. "We were on the last third of the train where we were least likely to get set off."

"I don't know exactly what happened," Collinwood said as he looked squarely at me, "but I'm pretty sure it was your fault." He smiled, took a long, thoughtful pause, and kicked into his stream-of-consciousness mode. "Okay, we're in Marion, and we've been set off on a siding. So we know trains stop here to set off and pick up. Questions are, how many a day? How often? And what direction? All we need is one train. Today. Going in either direction—to Indy or to Elkhart. We have several options here, but we are in a beautiful spot, and we could easily wait it out here until about six o'clock this evening, and if nothing by then, we still have enough daylight to consider other options."

I looked at the magnificent cemetery and the soft, green grass. "Sounds great to me," I concurred. I leaned back against my pack in the gentle morning sun. Collinwood had already begun telling stories about grade school music lessons and strange neighbors who leashed their young son to a stake in the front yard next to his boyhood home.

Later in the morning, I asked, "Did the grocery where you bought breakfast have a bathroom where I can wash up?" Collinwood hadn't checked but agreed to walk back over with me. In the restroom mirror, I could see that my hands and clothes were smudged with black grease from the boxcar floor. Under the mirror was a sink practically large enough to bathe in—and for a brief moment, I considered it.

After talking with the clerk, we changed our strategy. He told us that trains don't often come through more than once a day and that the chances were even less on Sunday. With the aid of a large city map on the grocery wall, we got our bearings, and, with packs and bedrolls in tow, we headed toward town in search of the Greyhound bus terminal. We heard a train whistle in the distance and ran optimistically to the track about a half-block ahead.

"Hey," Collinwood shouted, "maybe there's a freight coming through. Maybe we can catch it on the fly!" He sounded like a little boy proposing a dare.

I remembered a promise I'd made myself years ago. "Don't count on me. I won't jump a moving freight."

By this time, Collinwood realized that the freight we were hearing was on another track in a different part of town, but he persisted. "Let me show you how easy it would be." He ran down the track alongside an imaginary slowly moving train, acting out every step of his lesson. "First you see if you can keep up with it as you run, then you latch on to the grab iron on the front—never on the back—of the car, then you simply and *safely*"—he emphasized—"step up and on. Piece of cake." He finally "hopped" aboard his invisible train.

"Well, it's not my piece of cake," I bantered back.

"We need to get you comfortable with moving trains sometime on this trip," he concluded, too seriously to suit me.

During the long walk into town, I noticed that the little toe of my right foot was getting sore. "Maybe it's just my new boots," I thought. We discovered that Marion was deserted on Sunday. It was now late morning, and the only place that appeared to be open was the Catholic church, though Sunday Mass was over. Collinwood patiently agreed to sit out front and watch our packs while I made a short visit inside to pray for our safety and swift return to civilization. ("Dear Lord, a shower would be nice, too.")

As I was leaving, I noticed the priest sitting in a side room. I asked him if he could direct us to the town's rescue mission for a shower. I explained that we didn't need money, food, or a bed— just showers. He was sorry to tell me, but the mission allowed only men to shower, and even a phone call from the priest would not change their policy. Great balls of injustice! I can't pee out the boxcar door, and I can't shower at the mission. The priest detected my frustration and offered us the rectory shower. Mission accomplished!

Fresh bodies, fresh clothes, fresh spirits—and we were back on the road with the priest's directions to the bus terminal.

On the short walk, a young boy about twelve years old ran up alongside us. Laughing, he asked, "Hey, where you guys gonna build your fire?"

"Down by the river," Collinwood fired back amicably without missing a step.

Within moments, we were standing in front of the bus station. Just one problem: It was the *city* bus terminal. I waved down a carload of young guys going fishing. They said the Greyhound station had moved out by the interstate, fifteen or twenty miles away. As Collinwood crossed the street to get a closer look at an old Nickle Plate depot, I approached a car that had pulled up to the stop sign. The driver was a thin man with long, greasy strawberry blond hair and beard. He explained that Greyhound was actually on the far edge of town, and then he jumped out of the car and grabbed my pack off my back. "I used to do a lot of this shit myself," he mumbled. "Get in and I'll give you a ride." I called for Collinwood. The two of us and our gear filled the trunk and back seat. A fat, stringy-haired lady, probably the driver's wife or girlfriend, sat in the middle of the front seat with her left arm draped loosely behind her guy, and a wiry little old lady, probably related in another life to Jed Clampett, was wedged in against the passenger door.

On the long drive out of town, the driver related his Greyhound bus episodes to us, while the two ladies chatted simultaneously about food and babies. Collinwood and I, both recognizing that there was virtually no point in trying to exercise social skills in this situation, busied ourselves watching the miles of river and boardwalk for possible jungle sites in case the fickle finger of fate would keep us yet another night in Marion, Indiana.

Soon we found that our driver's knowledge of Greyhound was vast but outdated. He had taken us to the old location. As the young fishermen had told me earlier, the terminal had recently moved to the I-69 ramp—another ten miles away. "I sure don't want to leave you two stranded," our driver said, not really meaning it. He stopped to gas up, and after a twenty-minute drive along country back roads, Collinwood and I were eating egg salad sandwiches at the Greyhound Bus Terminal and Truck Stop and watching holiday traffic barrel down the interstate in the distance. It was not quite 2:00 P.M.

You can't get to Elkhart from Marion on a Greyhound bus without going back to Indianapolis. The cost of a ticket is sixteen dollars. That information registered the same question to both of us: Do we really want to spend sixteen dollars to go back where we were yesterday? We began to consider our other options.

With the help of a young clerk, I found a piece of cardboard that was just the right size, and Collinwood meticulously cut it into a large rectangle. As we sat at our booth finishing our drinks, Collinwood pulled a tube of black shoe polish from his pack and boldly lettered ELKHART on one side and FORT WAYNE on the other. At 2:45 P.M., we were standing at the end of the on-ramp, under a crisp blue sky, packs stacked neatly beside the highway, with Collinwood dauntlessly holding his boot-blacked sign high in the breeze. "Holy shit," I laughed aloud, "I don't even pick up hitchhikers, and now I am one!"

Collinwood began screaming to me over the loud din of traffic. "I have a philosophy about hitchhiking. Always face the drivers! Look interested! Pay attention! Act like you really want a ride!" Then he issued me a sort of warning. "You're gonna think I'm crazy, but I love this kind of shit. I really have fun with the drivers."

Suddenly, to my utter amazement, my mild-mannered, reserved, methodical, shy companion gave in to wild abandon. "Yoooo!" he screamed at the top of his lungs as a car approached at breathtaking speed. "Where ya going? Take us with ya!" And as it blew past us, he spun in the breeze and waved good-bye. "Maybe next time, eh?" Then he darted wildly into the highway and back, jumped up and down, spun around, and began to rant loudly again. Before I knew it, I was also waving at drivers, shouting, laughing, and snapping pictures.

Fun? Yes. Effective? I wasn't so sure. Nearly an hour had passed and still no ride. My little toe was getting progressively more irritated the longer I stood. "Collinwood," I asked, "how long will we keep trying—before we consider our other options?"

"We'll be in Elkhart by six," he said optimistically. I wasn't as hopeful, but my spirits were up, and I was enjoying the moment. I hadn't hitchhiked since I spent two years on the road as a nineteen-year-old hippie. Well, actually there was a time just a few years ago in the Andes Mountains during a trip with my son to Ecuador. What an adventure that was! Collinwood listened intently as I began telling the details of that experience. Mid-story, we heard a distant scream and looked behind us. Running up the highway toward us was a young woman, waving her arms and shouting to get our attention. "I'm trying to give you two a ride!" she screamed. "I thought I'd never get you to hear me!" Her van was parked quite a distance up the highway. Embarrassed, we grabbed our gear and ran alongside her to her van. So much for hitchhiking philosophy: Look interested, pay attention. We'd been so distracted that our kind driver actually had to run a quarter of a mile down the highway before we noticed her!

"I've been stranded before," she yelled as we ran toward her car. "Are you stranded? Is your car broken down?

"No, not really stranded," Collinwood answered breathlessly.

"I live nearly in Elkhart. I saw your sign and thought that it would be a shame not to give you a ride," she continued nonstop. "Are you moving to Elkhart? Is that why you're trying to get there?"

Wow, that last question was hard to believe. I thought, "Do we really look like two people *moving* to Elkhart? Sure, Collinwood has the sofa in his pack, and I've got the washer and dryer in mine!"

I screamed a promise in her direction: "We'll explain when we get in the van." She nodded her approval and continued running.

Riding down the highway, we learned that she worked for Fairmont Corporation, which makes mobile homes, and she lived in Nappanee, which was about twelve miles from Elkhart. Her younger brother was riding in the passenger seat. Collinwood was seated in the chair behind them, and I was in the back on the long bench. She was curious about us and began firing off questions. When I saw that Collinwood was doing fine responding, I whispered to him, "Is it okay if I sleep back here?"

"Not really," he muttered, "but go ahead." I knew that Collinwood was not joking. He had explained that some social situations were uncomfortable for him, and I was pretty sure this was a good example. I tried for a while to stay awake but could barely hear the conversation from the far back seat. Besides, the lack of sleep from the previous night was catching up with me. Half asleep and half awake, I picked up bits and pieces of conversation during more than two hours on the highway. I heard the driver say she planned to stop by her house in Nappanee, explain things to her family, and drive us into Elkhart.

Collinwood had speculated that we would be in Elkhart by 6:00 P.M. Our rescuer dropped us off in the parking lot of Taco Bell, which was only a couple of blocks from the Elkhart Yard, at exactly 5:55 P.M. Unbelievable!

To Graytown and Genoa, Ohio ("Golden Ways of Grain")

Elkhart put Collinwood on an adventure high. He knew these yards well and was excited at the prospect of jumping out here. While I ordered my food, he plunked quarters into the jukebox. We eagerly planned our strategy over burritos and Mexican pizza. In our enthusiasm, we were speaking more loudly than usual. A short, squatty man who had been sitting nearby with a woman approached us and asked, "You're not planning to jump freights outta here, are ya?" Realizing that he'd been listening in on our conversation, Collinwood admitted that we were considering it.

The lady walked up behind him as the man continued, "I work for the railroads, and I would suggest you think twice. It's easy to get into trouble in these yards." Collinwood explained that he was familiar with the Elkhart Yard, that he had jumped through there numerous times, and that he had even learned the hard way about the potential trouble here. The man continued to lecture us authoritatively for several moments. (Later we speculated that the lecture was for the benefit of his lady friend.) They turned to leave.

The woman had a two-day-old bouffant hairstyle and long purple nails. When she was far enough out the door so that she knew we would have little opportunity for a response, she blurted dramatically, "Don't you do anything to hurt any of those engineers. My brother's an engineer!"

Collinwood, as dumbfounded as I was at any implied violence, managed to respond humbly, "We really are nice people."

Our excitement somewhat subdued, Collinwood made a dash to the Subway shop next door for a veggies and cheese sub for the ride east and dug into a nearby dumpster for sufficient cardboard. We loaded up our packs and began the short walk toward the yard's fuel tanks.

When we turned at the next block, I spotted the little restaurant across from the yard where another hobo friend and I had staked out our catch on a freight trip to Toledo the previous October. It was also the restaurant from which Texas Madman had called me the day before Collinwood and I had begun our trip. Madman was hoping to head east toward Pennsylvania right after our phone conversation. Thinking that he might still be hanging around, we decided to hide our gear and come back to check for him. We proceeded west past the restaurant alongside the rails and dropped off the main road into a small alley because it was not yet dark enough to shadow us from railroad police and local officials. We finally cut across to the road, stashed our gear between two buildings, and hoped the clouds that had set in wouldn't soak everything before we returned. We walked back to the restaurant, used the restrooms, perused the tables and booths. There was no hint of Madman, so we returned to our gear.

We seated ourselves on a temporary rent-a-sign in front of a small auto repair business as the security of darkness settled upon us. After nearly an hour of scanner banter and no word of a departing train, the possibility of precipitation became a reality. "Would you like to do something I've always wanted to do but never have?" Collinwood challenged. I nodded reluctantly. He tried the doors on several of the old cars on the lot until he found one that was unlocked. We slipped into the front seat of a junked dark-colored Chrysler. My conscience was fast at work. Breaking and entering would be the charge if we were caught. But it was raining hard now, and we had no intention of damaging anything—and there were no other retreats. I reasoned myself out of guilt and watched as Collinwood, within mere seconds, drifted peacefully off to sleep behind the wheel. During the next couple of hours, two eastbound trains stopped to fuel up. I halfheartedly tried to rouse Collinwood, but he never completely awoke. I didn't push. After all, he had not napped as I had on the long ride to Elkhart in the van.

I nodded off and on until nearly 11:00 P.M., when I noticed Collinwood stretching. I began to talk, drawing him little by little out of his sleep and eventually out of our rubber-tired shelter. The rain had stopped. We entered the yard with our packs, climbed over several dead trains, and began to look for rides on trains that appeared to be made up for eastbound departure. We saw a grain car with a porch that had side walls and windows. On the front was a short solid wall as well. A grain car with an enclosed porch is rare to find. It was open sufficiently for scenery gawking but closed in enough for security. Collinwood went to search for clues and came back with a report. He had found a note tucked into the knuckle, a hinge of the coupling between railcars, at the front car. This train was bound for Pittsburgh and would be pulling out early in the morning. Wonderful!

We put down our cardboard and bedrolls and got out our snacks and water jugs. The sky had cleared and the stars, though somewhat dimmed by the Elkhart city lights, were faintly showing around us. I climbed down off the car to use the ballast bathroom before slipping into my bag for a few hours of peaceful rest before our departure east.

As we slept, Collinwood lay against the grain car with his head north; I was against the car's front wall with my head south. It was just before dawn that I woke to the pattering of rain on my bedroll. I looked at Collinwood, who was positioned back far enough that the rain was not yet reaching him. He was sleeping soundly. "It's raining," I whispered as I nudged him, "and we need the black plastic out of your pack." In a sleepy stupor, he reached into his pack and pulled out the plastic cover. I stretched it to reach across both bedrolls. Squinting his eyes, he asked, "Do you need anything else?"

"Well," I mumbled more to myself than Collinwood, "I don't really suppose there's anything else we can do other than use the plastic."

"Let me repeat myself." He sounded like a slow recording. "Is there anything else I can do for you?" I shook my head. "Good night," he said politely and pulled his bedroll closed again. Under the plastic, I slept well, waking only once to the sound of a yard worker walking in the gravel.

As dawn was breaking, I awoke again to a heavier drizzle and an unusually cool breeze. Our gear was getting wet, and rain was now trickling down the slanted front of the car and onto Collinwood. Our boots, which we had lined up along the front wall, were damp. Collinwood woke when he heard the rattling of the plastic. He was surprised that it was morning and that our train had not left. He listened to his scanner and explained that we would be departing soon. Within moments air was in the brakes. We had no time to even secure and hide our gear, let alone pack up and run for a boxcar where we would be sheltered from the now-steady rain.

"Get low and stay hidden until we're well out of the yard," Collinwood instructed, "and once we're clear, we'll get on our warmest clothes and rain gear." As the train gradually picked up speed, we were driven faster and faster into the cold rain. Once we were out of the yard, we hustled to yank on sweatshirts, coats, hats, gloves, and rain slicks, but each layer was getting wet before the next went on. Water was now standing in our boots, so we opted to stay in our stocking feet. We put our water-repellent foam cushion under us and shrouded ourselves in the black plastic.

Fifty, sixty, sixty-five miles an hour into cold pouring rain on the front end of a grain car! We fought the strong winds which continued to whip the plastic cover from around us. Within thirty minutes, my face felt raw and chapped. I remembered I still had some Chapstick hanging around my neck that I had used the day before to protect my lips from the intense sun as we had walked and hitchhiked. I fished it out through the layers of clothing and smeared it in heavy circles over my lips, cheeks, chin, and forehead.

The frigid downpour was relentless as we rolled out of Indiana and into Ohio. My body was becoming increasingly wet, painfully cold and stiff. I shifted from one side of my butt to the other, pressed my spine against the steel wall, and rolled my head from shoulder to shoulder for relief. My thin raincoat was ripping apart in the heavy wind. The hood of my army coat kept blowing away from my head, and my knit cap was becoming soggy. I felt chilly drops working their way down my neck and over the sensitive skin of my back. Our cardboard was saturated. By the time we rolled through the Toledo Yard, the floor of the grain car porch was filling up, the water level was up over the foam cushion on which we sat, and the bitterly cold puddle was soaking into my jeans and socks. Four hours had passed, and I tried not to think of the hours ahead of us to Cleveland.

"I'm beginning to shiver!" I shouted in Collinwood's direction.

Sensing my fear, he calmly replied, "That's a good sign. It's the way your body builds up its temperature." Emotionally, I felt reassured; physically, I ached.

I thought over and over, "Relax, sit still, stay calm." I looked occasionally at Collinwood. He looked miserable, too. I worked at keeping my mind busy and off my discomfort. I let the words of songs roll through my mind to the rhythm of the wheels—"Halle-lujah, I'm a Bum, Hallelujah Bum Again!" I recalled fragments of

"The Cremation of Dan McGee" and tried to remember which president died shortly after delivering his inaugural speech in a rainstorm. I conceptualized the details of my childhood home on DeQuincy Street in Indianapolis—the layout of rooms, placement of furniture, wall hangings, ashtrays, silverware drawer.

My mind game was interrupted by Collinwood, who was inching his way out of his black plastic. "The rain's letting up," he noted. I began to peel away layers of shredded rain gear. I poured the water out of my boots and tugged them onto numb feet. Collinwood began to reason, "We need to strip off any outer layers of wet clothes and allow the wind to dry us off."

"I'll freeze if the wind blows against my soaked clothes," I feared aloud, as I removed my dripping B.U.M. Equipment sweatshirt and tied it to the cable above my head. The floor of the grain car was littered now with discarded rain gear, wet clothing, hats, and gloves.

Collinwood grabbed hold of the cable on his side of the car and instructed me to grab on at my side. "Now, hold on and jump up and down in rhythm with the wheels," he ordered. "It may feel crazy, but it's a good way to build up some body temperature." Although I was now stripped down to my basic layer of clothing, within moments I was panting from the aerobic workout and was beginning to feel warm again. The stiffness left my limbs. We were cracking jokes, chuckling at ourselves, and waving at cars stopped at railroad signals. I grabbed my camera and snapped a picture of Collinwood, the railriding monkey, as he climbed daredevilishly off the fast-moving grain car and onto the tanker ahead of us.

As he made his way back onto our car, he noticed that our train had begun to slow down. "Maybe we're going to pull over onto a siding to let another train pass," he speculated optimistically. "That would be great because it would give us a chance to jump off this wide-open grain car and run back to something that would offer some protection from the rain, like a boxcar." Hopeful for such luck, we both began to pick up the wet, loose items on the floor. We stuffed them furiously into plastic bags, readying ourselves for a quick retreat.

The train had now slowed to less than ten miles per hour. We both were hoping our opportunity would present itself, when we heard a voice. A man who was standing at the street crossing ahead with a scanner in his hand was shouting at us. "You've been spotted; they're stopping the train; the police are coming; get off as fast as you can!" he managed to warn before we were carried out of earshot.

Immediately Collinwood was shouting his thoughts aloud. "We're too far from the yard, I believe, for them to dispatch railroad cops. They're probably sending city or county police. That's not good. A bull would probably just warn us; others will arrest us! The train's slowed down enough that we can jump off before they come." I nodded reluctantly. I certainly didn't want to be arrested, but neither did I care to jump off a moving freight. Collinwood saw me nod and began flinging our gear off the slowly moving train. He climbed down onto the grain car ladder and ordered me to climb down onto the one at the front end of the preceding tanker. We were about four feet from each other.

"Jump!" Collinwood shouted.

I had decided years earlier, when contemplating the possibility of my first freight ride, that I would *not* jump on or off a moving train—and as I assessed this situation, it didn't feel as though I was going to change my mind. "No," I answered firmly, "the train's moving too fast. I'm not going to jump."

Collinwood looked at me in disbelief, then he looked back at our gear, which was becoming more and more distant. "Look at the train now," he coaxed. "It's really slowing down. Will you jump now?" I shook my head. His voice had become high-pitched and tense. "Look at our gear, Gypsy! We'll never get back to it. We have hundreds of dollars worth of gear. Are you willing to lose it? The train's only moving about three miles per hour now. Will you jump off now?!"

"The gear's not as important as our safety, and I don't feel safe jumping off yet," I asserted.

Collinwood was squirming on the ladder, "I'm getting off!" he announced. "I really don't want to be arrested, and I don't want to lose my gear! The train's just creeping along, and I'm jumping off. Will you get off with me now?" I didn't answer. I was watching his feet to see if he would really carry out his threat.

To prove to me just how slowly the train was moving, he stepped off the train, then quickly jumped back onto the ladder. To my horror, I watched his left boot shift a bit on the wet step, then slip through the rung and against the flanged wheel! He yanked it back and miraculously regained his footing.

I gasped, "Collinwood, we can always get new gear; we can't grow new limbs! Please, it's not safe yet."

Glancing a final time at our gear, which was barely visible now, he glared at me and said in an angry but stiffly controlled voice, "Will you get off when the train STOPS? Will you get off THEN?!"

I had pushed his patience to the limit. It was time to exercise some courage. "Can you get off and run to catch up with me?" I asked. "Let me grab your hand, and I'll jump," I agreed halfheartedly. In a split second, he supported me as I hopped down.

We began the long, long brisk walk to our belongings, watching over our shoulders periodically for flashing red lights. By the time we reached our packs and plastic bags of gear, we could see a large grain elevator less than half a mile ahead. We ran for it, stashed our gear under a heavy blue tarp that was covering equipment, tucked in our shirts, and combed our hair. As the end of the train slowly inched its way past us, we casually walked across the track and into a small town, looking as though we had lived there all our lives. Reading the sign on the post office, we discovered that we were in Graytown, Ohio. The only restaurant in town—literally the only business in town—was closed for Labor Day, so we walked back to the tracks. No train, no police. Also, no highway, no public transportation, no people, no activity!

While we took time to think and examine our other options, we snacked, napped, changed clothes, and repacked. Then we faced the hard reality that only one option was open to us, and we exercised it: We walked! We passed again through

Graytown's greater metropolitan area—post office and restaurant—and began the long trek (an estimated ten or fifteen miles according to our map) to the Ohio Turnpike. The pain in my little toe was causing me to limp.

Shortly after we put our thumbs in the breeze, the angel of tired, wet, weary hobos with sore toes threw magic dust on us: An old man in a battered full-sized car pulled up alongside us. "Well, now, where y'all headed?" he asked in an animated sing-song voice.

"We're trying to get to the turnpike where we can hitch a ride," I explained as we climbed in with our load.

He asked the obvious question: "Well, now (every one of his sentences would begin with this phrase), what in creation are ya doing in Graytown?" Collinwood was seated in front and explained that we had a few days off, were doing a little unconventional traveling, and had been thrown off a train just outside this little town.

"Well, now, isn't that something. You're just a couple of adventuresome young people (I smiled at the last adjective!), just trying to see the country, trying to experience America—golden ways of grain and all that good stuff!" He nearly broke into song as he butchered up that last phrase—a phrase he was particularly fond of and would continue to repeat incorrectly at least a dozen times during our five-minute ride.

"Well, now, I love helping people out, and you two sure need some helping out, don't ya? Round here folks don't understand this free-spirit kind of thing. They understand farmin' and family and—golden ways of grain." Again he crooned the last phrase.

As he entered Genoa, the next small town, he pulled to a curb, and we gathered our gear. "Well, now, I sure wish ya both a good trip. The toll road's just a few more miles on up. I've gone a little out of my way to bring ya this far, but that's the American way, isn't it? Golden ways of grain and all that stuff!" We nodded a friendly thank you to our kind but marginally crazy driver and began to assess our options in this town. The good news—it was larger than Graytown. The bad news—it was just as dead.

Again, we exercised (literally!) our only reasonable option. We walked. And walked. And walked! Though we persistently employed Collinwood's master hitchhiking rules, the few drivers who passed us on this remote country roadway, which rolled monotonously through America's conservative corn belt, would not even make eye contact. During the four-hour trek, I actually felt invisible as driver after driver glanced the other direction or looked directly past us into the fields of soybeans and corn and golden "ways" of grain.

The sun was shining now, and my pack was rubbing uncomfortably against my perspiration-soaked sweatshirt. The small toe of my right foot was becoming more and more irritated with each mile of hiking. "How could something so small hurt so big!?" I thought to myself. My legs were shorter than Collinwood's, and consequently so was my gait. Even when I walked at the same pace, I would fall steadily behind. He stopped occasionally for me to catch up, and by the time I did, I felt guilty asking him to wait longer while I rested my painful back and toe. Two thoughts deterred me from wimping out. First, if I didn't continue walking, there were no other options. Obviously no one was going to pick us up—something in Genoa's air made us mysteriously invisible—and Collinwood certainly was not going to carry me. Second, I could now see the toll road ahead in the distance!

Once the Ohio Turnpike was in sight, we had two options. We could proceed the full two or three miles straight ahead and meet the highway at a ramp where we could hitchhike without technically encroaching on toll road property (very illegal!), or we could turn left and take a shortcut (about a mile and a half), meeting the highway at an overpass. If we took the shortcut, we would need to climb over a security fence, negotiate a steep embankment, and blatantly hitchhike on the toll road with the hope that a driver would pick us up before the Ohio highway patrol arrested us for trespassing. We checked the time. It was after 4:00 P.M., and daylight hours were running out. We opted for the shorter, more risky route.

Collinwood arrived at the overpass long before I and was sitting at the top in high weeds creating another shoe-polish masterpiece on a piece of cardboard he had picked up from someone's yard trash. Bold letters spelled out C L E V E. Collinwood found a spot where we could crawl under, rather than over, the fence. Then, slipping and sliding down the steep bank, we came to the pavement directly below and a few yards from the overpass that we had just crossed moments earlier.

The Ohio Turnpike, Oriental Style

We stacked our heavy belongings thoughtfully against a guardrail, hoping that it all wouldn't look so bulky to drivers. Traffic was flying by us. "Who in their right mind, and at the end of a long holiday weekend," I asked Collinwood, "would pick us up with this shitload of gear?"

He didn't smile but began his characteristic style of thinking aloud. "We may be in trouble here. It's dusk. Some people already have their headlights on. Our prime hitching time is about to run out. We may have an hour left at the most. Hopefully we won't be spotted by a trooper. If we don't get a ride before dark, here's the plan. We'll take turns—alternating every hour—sleeping under that overpass while the other holds our sign up into the headlights of oncoming traffic." He pointed at the narrow, flat platform at the top of the bridge's concrete understructure. I had seen homeless people asleep on ridges like that before and often wondered how they kept from rolling off the highly elevated twelve- or fourteen-inch ledge in their sleep. I shuddered to think that I might learn the answer to that question firsthand in less than a few hours! I had never thought it possible to hitchhike at night, but now Collinwood was considering it as a viable option. I prayed for a ride; Collinwood held our sign.

It was about fifteen minutes later when I noticed that every passing auto had headlights on. I began to prepare myself for the grim reality of unanswered prayer and the horrors of slumber ledge. But as the case had been time and time again, our need would be met. A brand-new silver Chrysler van was pulling over. By the time its driver managed to separate himself from the heavy, speeding traffic, he was a long distance up the highway. In a flash Collinwood had his pack on and was running toward the answer to our prayer. The driver was the middle-aged father of a large Japanese family that filled the vehicle. The mother was sitting in the passenger seat holding the youngest child, a boy about two years old. Three children who had been sitting on the short second bench obligingly squeezed themselves in among three older boys on the long back bench, obviously clearing the short bench for us and our ton of gear. We awkwardly packed ourselves in. Our new traveling companions watched silently.

As the van pulled away, the mother looked me squarely in the eyes, nodded, and smiled as if to say, "Relax, dear, everything is okay now."

In years of international travel, I had never appreciated as I did at this moment that smiles are, indeed, a universal language. The smile I returned to her was meant to convey a message as clear as the one I had just received: "Thank you, kind mother and compassionate sister, for rescuing me—tired back, sore toe, weary spirit, and all—from the horrors of slumber ledge, from the cold night road, from the state troopers, and from the indifference and mediocrity of places like Graytown and Genoa." I somehow believe she understood.

After a couple of mute moments, the father looked deliberately into the rearview mirror to catch the eye of his eldest son. On cue the boy leaned forward between me and Collinwood and asked softly in broken English, "How—long—you—were—standing—there?"

Collinwood replied, "Oh, we were there for about twenty minutes, I guess."

The insecure tone of the boy's English broke into strong, bold Japanese as he reported Collinwood's response to his family. Suddenly the van filled with chaotic shouts of conversation. Everyone was shrieking furiously in Japanese at the same time. The din continued for a good two minutes, then gradually tapered off until the last comment had been voiced.

Again there was stark silence before the young family-appointed interviewer leaned up again, "Where—you—from?" Collinwood paused, giving me a chance to answer this one. I couldn't budge. I was absolutely ready to burst into uncontrollable laughter. To avoid such a scene, I held my nose and shut my mouth tightly to prevent any sound from escaping. My ears began to pop. Collinwood glared at me in disgust as he answered with amazing self-control. "I'm from Cleveland, and my friend here is from Indianapolis, Indiana." A repeat performance followed again and again. Report, loud Japanese discussion, silence, and next question.

Eventually I regained my composure, and during the hundred-mile ride to Cleveland, I observed this lovely family. They were tastefully dressed in designer wear, the children were exemplary, the parents were calm and patient, even with the youngest child squirming endlessly on his mother's lap. And they all were remarkably at ease and comfortable with the two unusual vagabonds they had invited to join their family circle. They politely dropped us off in Cleveland at the West 98th and Detroit rapid-transit station. There we boarded our train to Collinwood's back door.

From Trash to Treasures

It was 8:20 P.M. as we climbed the stairs of Collinwood's two-story house, ascending past the basement and first floors, which were stacked to the ceiling with years of dumpster-diving treasures, and on up to the second-floor living quarters. He had fairly warned me, but I was bewildered by the heaps of accumulation. We plopped down our packs, and he gave me a grand tour, beginning back in the basement and ending upstairs.

The upper floor where he lived was as cluttered as the lower ones. The difference was that this floor had a much higher quality of trash pickings, and they were meticulously organized and labeled. The walls of the kitchen were solidly filled with an abundance of canned and boxed goods, each marked with the date of purchase. Boxes that were overflowing with neatly washed cat food cans and plastic storage containers lined the walls. "Surely I'll find a scout troop or church group someday that wants to use those for a craft project," he speculated. A narrow path led the way to the bathroom, his bedroom, his computer space, and the living room. Plastic tubs and cardboard boxes were appropriately marked: tea, pencils, shirts, rubber bands, markers, coupons, film, string and tape, and numerous other labels. Hundreds of CDs and VCR tapes covered various walls, and he had created catalog after catalog listing each one according to the artist or title in alphabetical order. Cracked and faded white walls were decorated with pencil sketches, posters, postcards, and letters. A rubber bat hung from the ceiling over his computer and was growing elaborate cobwebs. A free-verse poem titled "A Real Thanksgiving" had been typed and printed on his computer and taped to the wall behind his work area. Lights, speakers, TVs, and scanners had been thoughtfully rigged up in every room, leaving behind a chaotic network of wires and cords.

Clutter has rarely been a part of my life—order gives me a feeling of security and safety—but within minutes I was as comfortable as the two resident cats, Spot and Justin. After a dinner of spaghetti served with Collinwood's homemade vegetarian sauce, I took a bath. By midnight, I shoved small mounds of carefully sorted "stuff" aside. ("Don't knock over any of those stacks!" I'd been warned.) I laid my sleeping bag down in a small clearing on the living room floor and fell asleep watching a Prime Time video starring our friend Road Hog. Collinwood slept in his bed for the first time in four nights.

I woke the next morning when Collinwood stepped over me to go out a door and onto the second-floor porch. We enjoyed tea and egg sandwiches in the fresh cool air while I watched a neighborhood squirrel carry nut after nut across a thick telephone cable beside the porch. Collinwood had lowered it a year earlier, without permission, to clear the view of the railroad and transit tracks that run alongside his house. We talked about family, jobs, trips, philosophies, and the purchase of his older East Cleveland home. (At $8,000, it was like trash-picking to get it!) It began to drizzle, and we both agreed, after the previous day's soaking, to forgo additional adventure if it didn't clear up. I called to check bus fares back to Indianapolis just in case the rain had set in for the day. Within a couple of hours, however, the sun was breaking through the clouds.

We threw wet clothes in the dryer without bothering to wash them, reorganized our packs, and left Collinwood's trash-to-treasures abode. We were headed for the Collinwood Yard—destination unknown.

On the Road Again

It was early afternoon when we pulled out of Collinwood's drive. On the way to the yard, he pointed to a few East Cleveland points of interest—drug dealers and their hot corners (one of which was at the end of his block), historic buildings, and parks. We drove from one end of the Collinwood Yard to the other, then stopped at a fruit market and deli to pick up lunch, which we would eat at Collinwood's jungle.

He had set up his jungle near the yard, so it could be used by railriders passing through. There were a fire ring, a table, chairs, cooking utensils, and rules which had been posted for those using it. At one time he had kept it supplied with food, but in early August, a copy of one of Collinwood's railriding journals had fallen into the hands of the captain of the railroad police force. In addition to other private bits of information, the journal disclosed the jungle site. The railroad police were ordered to tear it down. What remained was in shambles, but we sat peacefully amid the ruins eating our cheese sandwiches while Collinwood listened to his scanner, hoping for a train "highballing" east.

"Son of a bitch!" Collinwood laughed at what he was hearing on his scanner. "Do you want to go home? The first damn train heading out is the BUIN (Buffalo to Indianapolis), a good three hours early! Wanna take it?"

I sure hadn't expected to head back west. "How long will it be in the yard?" I asked, trying to figure how much time we had to make up our minds.

Collinwood's answer didn't help. "Could be fifteen minutes; could be four or five hours."

We decided to finish our lunch before making a decision. If it left without us, it just wasn't meant to be. After all, we really didn't have a destination. Just as we were cleaning up our trash to leave, Collinwood said, "Well, that's not an option anymore. The BUIN just got clearance for departure."

"Is it actually pulling out right now?" I asked.

Collinwood said, "It'll probably be a minute or two. Wanna go watch it pull out? Hell, there's even a slim chance that we'll be able to get on it!"

We ran to his car and sped the few blocks to the catch-out point at the east end of the yard. There sat the BUIN, a mixed freight, ready to depart. Collinwood pulled into a parking spot behind a building where he felt comfortable being parked for a few days. We jumped out to grab our packs from the hatchback, but before we put them on our shoulders, the train began to move. "Oh, well," Collinwood reflected, "I never get upset about missing trains anymore. There'll be other options this afternoon."

We got back in his car, intending to overtake the train so that we could watch it, in its entirety, pass by us at an intersection several blocks away. We were about to pull out of the lot when Collinwood slowed to a stop. He lifted his right index finger to his lips, knitted his brow thoughtfully, and paused a moment before speaking. "Do we want to catch that train? We can catch that train if we really want to. Hang on, Gypsy Moon, we're catching the BUIN!" He explained that the chances were excellent that this train would stop at Rockport, about twenty miles from the Collinwood Yard, to pick up a section of cars. Chances also were excellent that we could beat it. "In fact," laughed Collinwood, "I'll bet you that we can drive into downtown Cleveland, wave at the crew as they cross over the drawbridge, and still get to Rockport in time to catch out!"

The drive was outrageous. "Get out of the way!" Collin-wood screamed at drivers at the onset of rush-hour traffic. "Can't you see we've got a train to catch?! Move it! Move it!" Traffic became heavy as we entered downtown Cleveland, and though we were having an outlandish time pushing our luck, Collinwood continually checked his watch. We made it to the bridge about five minutes before the train.

Collinwood dashed across the tracks and into some high weeds to answer nature's call. I studied the massive steel struc-ture. I had never seen a drawbridge like this one before. The term, I decided, is a misnomer; it should be called a lift bridge since, rather than drawing apart and opening, it actually lifts to allow room for boats to clear. Collinwood returned in time for us to wave wildly at the conductor and engineer as the train barreled toward the overpass, then we ran to his car to continue what now had become a ludicrous nose-to-nose race.

As Collinwood reached for the car door, he gasped. He had left his billfold in the weeds. He might not have realized it until it was too late, had it not been for an unusual safety measure he had taken. As he had squatted in the high brush, he removed his billfold from his pants and set it aside. Concerned that in the excitement he would forget to pick it up, he placed his car keys atop it. The precaution worked. He couldn't leave for Rockport without his car keys—which were with his wallet. He darted off. Valuable seconds were ticking away as he retraced his steps across the tracks and back to his car.

The swift drive to Rockport ended as we pulled into the rapid-transit park-and-ride lot, another excellent place to park for a few days. Laden with our gear, we climbed a guardrail and ran under an overpass. There sat a Department of Transportation van under the bridge and our train on the tracks! There was no choice now but to be bold and fast. We ran blatantly past the van as the engines were backing just yards in front of us and continued on down the tracks alongside the section of train waiting to be picked up momentarily. We came to a boxcar, and I stopped to throw my gear aboard.

"No, no! Let's run farther back and look for another one," Collinwood panted. "If they saw us, they'll probably come to check the first or second good ride, then hopefully they'll give up." We continued to the third good ride—a boxcar with a door open on each side—and jumped on. Within ten minutes we were bound for Indianapolis.

Collinwood pointed out sights as we rolled out of the metropolitan area and again as we passed through his childhood hometown of Berea. He noted an abandoned railroad battery box at a Berea intersection. It had a padlock on it. "Everyone thinks it's a railroad lock," Collinwood smiled, "but it's mine. When I'm in Berea, it's my own personal locker!"

I had never been on a moving freight during the day. It was a splendid, sunny midafternoon in September, and Ohio was showing off for us. One small town after another gave way to pastures of horses and cattle and sheep; fields of corn and soybeans and wheat; fencerows of brown-eyed daisies and sunflowers. A faded Mail Pouch message on the side of a weathered old barn hinted at another season—a phase in history when there were visible gas pumps, five-and-dime stores, soda fountains, and steam engines.

This weekend I had felt mystically suspended between seasons—between a phase of my life that is rooted, responsible, and predictable and a new phase that is unbridled, detached, and serendipitous. Listening to the rhythm of the steel wheels, I pondered the tempo of my life. The temperature was gently dropping, so I pulled on my down vest. Stretching out on my bedroll near the door, I watched dusk bring new colors to the heartland. Yellow corn tassels turned to orange; soft green pastures changed to gray.

Collinwood walked over and nudged me. "Come to the other side and see the sunset." What a treat it was to have doors open on each side of the car! While the sky I had been watching from the south door was clear and blue, the western horizon seen from the north door was scattered with clouds. The sun had dipped behind them, and beams of yellow, blue, and charcoal were cutting through and bursting wildly earthward. I was re-minded of an old religious print that hung years ago in my Aunt Marie's dining room. It showed Christ descending through clouds that created the same magnificent sunburst. I grasped the boxcar strap and leaned out against the wind, watching steadily as the clouds dispersed and the sun sank and the beams gave up their luster. We were on the last leg of our trip home.

The night sky was subtle compared to the star-studded magnificence of our first night's ride to Marion. There was no moon until long after we had arrived in Indianapolis. As towns drifted by in the darkness, Collinwood watched for illuminated building or road signs to match against his map. From time to time, he gave a report: the state line, Pendleton, Interstate 69. Each marked the need to shift mental gears. The steel rails that had carried me away to no specific destination were now return-ing me dead-center to the responsible, predictable phase of my life that awaited me in southern Indiana.

Return to the Avon Yard

Rolling back into Indianapolis at night was like being part of a movie run in reverse of our first night's ride. Indy lights became more and more intense, illuminating charming inner-city neighborhoods and downtown landmarks: the Old East Side, Fountain Square, the Eli Lilly facility, and the municipal airport.

It was nearly midnight as our train reached its termination point in the Avon Receiving Yard. A heavy network of trains filled the many tracks to the north of ours. To the right were four unoccupied tracks, a gravel yard road, several more empty tracks on the other side of that road, and finally a stack train standing without power on the southernmost track. To avoid being seen, Collinwood and I stood at opposite sides of the open door, pressed against the south wall with our respective gear at our sides. Bodies and packs out of sight, we craned our necks to survey the conditions for escape. Collinwood had a better view to the front of the train, since he stood farther to the back of the car. I was relieved that the yard south of us, which I could see plainly, appeared to be clear except for the single stack train. It looked like an easy end to our trek: The train would stop, we would dart across the gravel road and empty tracks, over the stack train, and onto the paved road that would lead us back to the shopping plaza where my car waited.

My optimism was pierced by Collinwood's shout: "Get back! Here comes a truck."

I jumped back as our train came to a stop. Even from a distance, the approaching headlights brightened the inside of our car. I tugged at my gear, fearing it could be within the beams' reach, and I held my breath waiting for the slowly moving vehicle to pass. Then, to my dismay, it stopped—right in line with the door of our car! Leaving the truck running, the driver got out. We could see the bright shaft from a flashlight swaying from side to side as he crunched through the gravel directly toward our door. My body was pressed fearfully against the steel wall. My eyes were on my belongings, which were piled up between me and the door. So far my gear had remained in the shadows, but how much closer would those lights come? When the man was only a few feet from the door, he stopped. He scanned the interior of our car with his light. I took a deep breath and shut my eyes. I could feel my heart pounding inside my boots. I breathed a sigh of relief as I heard him turn and walk toward the back of our car to unhook the hoses. The overdose of adrenaline caused me to feel faint.

Collinwood tiptoed over to me and touched my arm. With a grin in his voice, he whispered, "I just love this shit!" He continued teasing. "He left his truck running; wanna take it?" We walked swiftly to the far north corner to hide again as the man walked past the other door to unhook the next set of hoses. After several minutes, we heard the truck door slam, and the man with the flashlight was gone.

My legs were rubber as I listened to Collinwood reason aloud. "Although the tracks are pretty clear to the south of us, there's just too much activity up ahead: trucks, lights, yard crew. We could make a mad dash across the yard and over that stack train, but we'll probably be spotted. If, on the other hand, we get off on the north side of this train, we have another stationary train on the track beside us. We can get a good part of the walk out of the way hidden between these two trains. In fact, we may be able to walk all the way to the front of our train, then just walk around it rather than climb back over it."

My heart still had not returned to its normal rate, so I readily agreed to take the route with the least chance of being caught. We climbed down, loaded our packs onto our backs, and began walking westward in the shadow of the two trains toward the heart of the yard. The train beside us ended about three car lengths before the front of ours. We peeked around it and could see that the numerous yard buildings were within two hundred feet. If we did try to walk around the front of our train as we had planned, we would run a high risk of being seen. Ducking back into the shadows to consider our options, we heard an engine. It was another train backing in at an angle across the front of the two trains to our sides.

"Look!" Collinwood called. "This train's going to end up between us and the buildings. If we move fast, we can get around our train and out of the yard during the few minutes we're shielded from view."

At the appropriate second, Collinwood darted into the lights of the yard. I followed. Just as we began to turn in front of our train, I spotted a yard worker through the opening of an empty lumber car. He was standing on the opposite side of the moving train. "Stop, Collinwood!" I warned as I ran back into the shadows. Collinwood followed.

Now we could see the end of this third train, which was creeping slowly diagonally between us and the buildings. Time was running out. We decided to retreat about three or four cars and advance over our train rather than walk around the front. Just as we climbed over the couplers of our dead train the moving one passed, leaving us again exposed to the activity just a short way up the yard. There was no choice now but to dash boldly across the yard.

But in a split second, before we had a chance to run, lights of an oncoming engine hit us. "What the hell!" Collinwood screamed. "Hide between cars!" We turned and dove headfirst between the nearest two cars of our dead train, hoping that our dark clothes and packs would be camouflaged in the night. The engine pulled fifty or sixty cars of its long mixed freight past us before stopping. Neither end of the long train was in sight. We now had a new obstacle in front of us. Collinwood suggested that we retreat another five or six cars and cross over this new mixed train.

The idea frightened me. "It's live, Collinwood. What if it lunges forward as we cross?"

He answered my question with another question: "What are our options?"

By looking under the train and between the cars, we could see that a flurry of activity had begun on the other side. Trucks and cars were moving up and down the gravel road. We hid behind wheels each time headlights passed. "Not good!" Collinwood gasped, as he saw the words *Railroad Police* on the side of one of the vehicles. "Where the hell are all these people going this late at night, to a damned convention? Son of a bitch, we'll never get out of here!"

In all of the confusion, we heard the roar of another engine. This time it was a pig train (consisting of flatbed cars loaded with semitrailers) headed east on the track on the other side of the mixed train. A fairly lengthy section of it passed before it stopped. A second obstacle! Without any discussion, I followed Collinwood over the couplers of the live mixed freight, fearing every second that its powerful double engines would jerk it into motion. After we were safely on the other side, there was again just one obstacle— the pig train—separating us from the heavy activity that continued up and down the gravel road. "The problem here," Collinwood explained, "is that this pig train is carrying mail." (It had been identified on his scanner as "Mail 4.") "It's a high-security train, and we're in a high-security area of the yard near the . . . " He stopped mid-sentence. "Shit!" he screamed. "Here comes a railroad cop with a spotlight! Stay down!" We bent behind the flanged wheels of the mail train and hid from the spotlight, which slowly scanned its bright glare across trailer after trailer.

"Damn, I don't believe it. This train's moving again." Collinwood was bewildered. The pig train was our only shield from the road. Realizing that we would be in full view after it passed, we disregarded the danger once again and climbed back over the live mixed freight.

As we walked again toward the heart of the yard, we could see that, just as before, the activity was becoming heavier and heavier. It was beginning to look as if there was no way out. Collinwood stopped abruptly. He threw his head back in frustration. Silence. There was no need to speak. We each knew the score. We had been taxed to the limit; we were physically and emotionally exhausted. I just wanted this dreadful ordeal to end—at any cost. I felt that I would actually thank a railroad cop for arresting us at this point. Sounding as crazy to myself as I did to Collinwood, I asked, "What's preventing us from simply walking into that building and turning ourselves in?"

Collinwood didn't laugh. His response reflected my attitude of resignation: "Let's just go for it. Get it over with. What the hell, if we're caught, we're just caught. Try to keep up."

His steps were rapid and constant as we fled. I kept up. Across track after track, across the gravel road, across more tracks. Coming to a ravine, Collinwood shouted, "This ditch is muddy and deep, but don't slow down!" I didn't. Thick mud made my boots heavy as we continued across the remaining rails and slippery as we climbed awkwardly over the stack train. I slipped as we scrambled up the embankment to the gravel road which led us in full view of several yard buildings. "We're still on railroad property," Collinwood warned as we came to a long asphalt road busy with semitrailer trucks and pickups. "If we've been spotted, a railroad cop will be driving up any minute."

It seemed like an eternity before we reached the paved

road leading to my parked truck. "Home free! Off railroad property!" Collinwood proclaimed as he stomped his feet on the highway, loosening a heavy accumulation of mud from his boots.

"Thank you, Lord!" I screamed. "This is a public road, a thoroughfare, a municipal right-of-way. It actually belongs to me, a citizen, a taxpayer, a Hoosier!" I was elated to be back, to be safe, to have my feet on solid, legal ground again. I momentarily understood why people long separated from their homelands kiss the ground upon their return; yet at the same time, I was exhilarated by the adventure we had endured.

"Collinwood," I reflected as we walked, "I can't say it's been the best time I've ever had. It was really tough at times. But it certainly has been the most memorable."

"That's great to hear," he answered. "I have more than two weeks off in October. That's enough time to travel a good distance, maybe to California and back. I've never gone across country on freights. Always wanted to."

"All right!" I shrieked without hesitating.

During the mile walk back to my truck, I recalled the words of an old Tom Paxton song that warns anyone wishing to be a rambler. "Nail your shoes to the kitchen floor, lace 'em up and bar the door."

"Too late, Gypsy Moon," I whispered. "Too late!"

Taco Bell was open until 1:00 A.M., and we were barely in time to place the last order of the day at the drive-through. As we sat in the front seat of the truck eating bean burritos, we excitedly considered the plans for our next trip.

We drove back to the yard, and for the next five hours we wearily worked at getting Collinwood on a freight back to Cleveland. He finally jumped aboard an eastbound at 7:30 A.M. I made the hour's drive back to the hills of Brown County, back to my fuzzy little pup Moon Shadow, and back to my log cabin in the woods, where I called a podiatrist to schedule next-day surgery on my little toe. That night, in my own bed once again, I drifted off to sleep dreaming of California-bound freights.

That week after my return, cool temperatures set in earlier than usual. The hills were becoming dormant; small animals were burrowing down to hibernate, and large ones were wearing thicker coats. As I watched the forests around my lake transform into an autumn wonderland, I became keenly aware of the cyclical nature of my own life.

Hot Off the Jungle Fires:
Hobo Recipes

Menus in the jungle are as interesting as the folks who prepare them. Nothing compares to a battered old tin cup of steamy hobo stew served up hot and hearty along the tracks. Hobos are resourceful and capable when it comes to a gun boat or a makeshift griddle. A few of the more renowned and adept have agreed to share some favorite recipes. This was a challenge since recipes don't really exist in jungles. Hobos cook as unconventionally as they live. The general rule: "Take what you got. Put it in a pot. Cook it 'til it's hot. And they'll eat it or not!"

Confessions of a Tramp Cook
by Snapshot

Because somewhere along his life's journey Snapshot had worked as a chef, I requested a recipe for the best chili I'd ever eaten. However, you don't always get from a hobo that which you request. I received the following.

I have been asked repeatedly for my "famous" chili recipe, served to hobos and guests at the Indiana Transportation

Museum's Annual Hobo Days in Noblesville, Indiana. Confession: I had never made chili before this occasion and have never made it since. Nevertheless, here for posterity is my "secret" recipe.

Caboose Chili

Take chili ingredients in sufficient quantities and combine in proportions pleasing to the palate. Cook until done. Serve hot. (Eat with tongue in cheek.)

A hobo carries his recipes in his head, not neatly transcribed on three-by-five cards. I have yet to meet the hobo cook who has stashed away in his pack a copy of *The Joy of Cooking!* It most often isn't a question of how you're going to cook something, but what that something will be. You eat what is close at hand and in season.

Also, the phrase "cooking from scratch" probably originated in the hobo jungles. Many a time, a Knight of the Road could be seen scratching while cooking—what with mosquitos, chiggers, poison ivy, etc.

Hints from Snapshot

Hint #1: Soap the outside of the pot before using it to cook over an open fire. When finished, the soot will rinse off easily.

Hint #2: The oldtime hobos talk of the days of steam as though they were a thing of the past. Let's lay this myth to rest once and for all. Steam is still the preferred alternative to grease, butter, or lard, any of which can melt or turn rancid in your bindle. Water is usually available. To prepare fish, meats, or vegetables, simply place on a wire grid over a pot of water, and set over the campfire. Steam 'til tender. This method of cooking not only locks in the flavorful juices, but the valuable nutrients as well. An added bonus: cleanup is fast and easy.

Fry Pan Jack's Gastronomical Extravaganza

by Minneapolis Skinny

The following account by Minneapolis Skinny describes the inge-
nuity of a hobo cook.

Eighteen years ago in Britt, on an early Sunday morning
in August, Fry Pan Jack cooked up a breakfast for his departing
hobo comrades. From that memorable experience, I learned how
he got his famous moniker and why he is the undisputed crumb
boss of America's jungle kitchens.

Even the veterans of the cinder trail who were waiting to
get their last hot meal before heading out were awed by Jack's
jungle fire prowess. Connecticut Slim, Slow Motion Shorty, Vir-
ginia Slim, Steamtrain Maury, Easy Money, Lord Open Road,
Cheyenne Kid, Big Town Gorman, and the Pennsylvania Kid
were in the hungry crowd that day. Three gun boats of water were
put on to boil: one for the ever-present pot of coffee, one for
potatoes, and one for boiled eggs. Jack's frying pans were ready in
his bindle, oiled and scoured clean, so the onlookers were resigned to the common fare of boiled eggs, potatoes, and coffee.
But Fry Pan took better care of his comrades that morning. After
all, as Jack was about to prove, who can improvise better than a
hobo?

Seeing several fifty-gallon drums behind a nearby printing
office, Jack quickly liberated a drum lid and proceeded to heat it—
slowly enough that it would not warp, yet hot enough to bake off
the paint and residue. When it had cooled, he scrubbed it with
gravel, then with sand and soap, then rinsed it thoroughly. He put
it back on the fire and got the temperature just right before
covering this monster griddle with cooking oil. While the bewildered onlookers watched in amazement, Jack sautéed onions,
garlic, and green peppers on part of his thirty-six-inch fry pan. In
another section he fried hamburger and sausage. In a third area

he diced the partially boiled potatoes. He eventually brought all the ingredients together at the center and finally diced the hard-boiled eggs, which he sprinkled carefully on top of his gastronomical extravaganza.

He turned his attention then to his famous jungle coffee: one-third handful of salt in the boiling water, followed by four handfuls of grounds and one egg. A clean spike, placed across the top of the pot, kept the brew from boiling over.

Never before, nor since, had I witnessed such a group of hobos as the ones there that morning. Their reverence for a master at work spoke clearly of the respect Jack had established among his peers as America's number one hobo cook!

The Thirsty Hobo (Drinks)

Hobo Coffee—Steamtrain Style

Many a hobo has talked a restaurant out of used coffee grounds because hobos know that grounds used only once still have "life" in them. Back in the jungle, they are cooked slowly over the fire in a tin can of water into a fine hobo coffee. A long nail or railroad spike resting over the top of the can keeps the coffee from boiling over.

Substitute Hobo Coffee—Reefer Charlie Style

When no coffee is available, try what the hobos have substituted: dandelion roots! Dry the roots, then roast them in a skillet over the fire until they are dry and very brown. Crush them to the texture of ground coffee and perk. Reefer recommended this simply as a good substitute for coffee or as a blood purifier and treatment for gout and rheumatism.

Snapshot's Bum-Toddy

apple cider	dash of allspice
dash of cinnamon	dash of nutmeg
a little spirit (to taste!)	

Combine ingredients in pot and steep over a few hot coals. Amount of spirits, of course, should be added in direct proportion to the coolness of the evening and the medicinal need.

Sassafras Tea—Reefer Charlie's Favorite

Cut a root off about three or four inches from the base of the sassafras tree. One cut like this will not hurt the tree if you tamp the soil back over the root stub. Wash and scrub root with water only. With a knife, remove the bark of the root and spread it on paper to dry. It will keep indefinitely. The bark can often be boiled twice for tea. Only the bark of the root is used for tea.

Hobo Convention Specials
by Steamtrain Maury

A visit to Britt's hobo jungle at convention time would not be complete without Steamtrain's famous hobo stew.

Steamtrain's Hobo Stew

20 lb. beef roast (lean), cut into 1" cubes	2 large bottles of soy sauce and 1 bottle of Louisiana Hot Sauce
30 lb. potatoes, cubed	
30 lb. carrots, sliced	4 to 5 large cans of tomato sauce
5 lb. onions, diced	
2 to 3 bundles of stalk celery, diced	garlic powder
	salt and pepper
3 heads of cabbage, cubed	1 lb. margarine
1 to 2 gallon cans of green beans	several bay leaves (fish out before serving!)

1 to 2 gallon cans of kernel corn   4 lb. plain (no additives)
Durkee's Italian Herbs   yellow cornmeal

Begin boiling 1 gallon of water in a large pot over an open fire. Add meat, lifting off all bubbly foam with a skimmer while cooking until remaining broth is clear. Add vegetables, tomato juice, and margarine (add potatoes thirty or forty minutes before stew is done). Cook, stirring occasionally, with a fresh, peeled, sturdy branch. After a couple of hours, add other vegetables. Cooking slowly, add water as needed until vegetables are done. Add soy sauce and remaining seasonings to taste. Allow to simmer another 30 minutes or so. Finally, thicken by slowly sprinkling (with sifter) yellow cornmeal into stew until it is at desired thickness, stirring constantly to avoid sticking on pot's bottom. Serve, leaving just enough coals under the pot to keep it hot through the serving period. Serves 200. Enjoy!

Steamtrain—About Yellow Cornmeal

It was a miracle food. When times were hard, even the poorest could afford cornmeal, also called maize. During the Great Depression, it kept millions from starving because the quantity of soup or stew or chili could be nearly doubled by adding cornmeal—and the taste was great. Cooked as mush, a pound could feed several. It could either be added to the pot, as in the hobo stew recipe, or cooked, allowed to set up, cut into small squares, and added to the pot near the end of cooking. When stirred, the chunks would thicken the food by only partially dissolving, leaving small, soft lumps of cornmeal behind.

Steamtrain's Sunshine Pickles

Many youngsters over the years have spent an August afternoon during the convention "spearing" Sunshine Pickles, using a tiny stick that Steamtrain cleaned and sharpened for them.

1 gallon jug or coffee can   1/2 gallon water
1 clean bandana   1/2 gallon vinegar
1 large onion   1 small jar of pickling seeds
1 gallon of cucumbers, sliced

Put sliced cucumbers (the thickness of hamburger pickles) and thinly sliced onion into container. Fill with equal parts of water and vinegar. Add pickling seeds, cover with a clean bandana to keep bugs out, and set in the sun for two days. Small twigs, cleaned and pointed, can be used for spearing and eating.

Carefree and Southern
by Carolina Coley

Born in 1898, Carolina Coley (the author's father) prepared simple and tasty meals influenced by his southern background.

Southern Kale and Turnips

1/2 lb. bacon, diced   ham bone
1 medium onion, diced   salt and pepper to taste
1 bundle of fresh kale   vinegar
4 large turnips, cubed

Brown bacon pieces and onion. Move bacon and 4 tbs. of bacon grease to a large pot. Add cleaned kale, turnip cubes, ham bone, and salt and pepper to taste. Add enough water to almost cover. Cook until vegetables are soft. Dish out and serve with vinegar.

Fishin' for Pigeon

by Buzz Potter, editor of the Hobo Times,[*]
a magazine for, about, and by hobos

Creamed Squab à la Jungle

Pigeons were and still are ubiquitous denizens of freight yards, especially around grain elevators or tracks that hold grain cars. Such places always "leaked" a few grains, making nourishing and fattening bird food. Pigeons are pretty oblivious to humans, and if a guy is real quick, he can catch one by hand or dispatch one with a lucky rock throw. Some hobos would carry a drop line which consisted of a fifty-foot length of fishing line, a sinker or two, and a small hook attached. We'd wrap the whole thing around a short stick and stash it in our bedroll against a time when we'd jungle up near a lake or stream. It was easy to catch small sunfish or bullheads that made pretty good eating, but the fish line was also a deadly tool for catching pigeons. We'd bait the hook with anything from a piece of soda cracker to a bright shred of cloth and place it among a concentration of scattered grain. Within minutes, the pigeons would come to see what we'd left them. The rest is obvious; we'd just reel them in and wring their necks.

Now pigeon, in some social circles, is a real epicurean delight. It has dark meat like a grouse or pheasant and tastes fairly similar to both. In pricey restaurants, it's advertised as *squab* and exquisitely prepared in a cream sauce with mushrooms and pearl onions. But alas, in jungles we didn't have such luxuries as cream sauce, so we improvised to come as close as possible. Just thinking of it makes me want to cook up a pigeon stew like I did in the old days. As I remember, it was absolutely, sinfully delicious.

5-6 pigeons	celery or carrots
quartered onions	3 tbs. cornstarch or flour
unpeeled wedges of potatoes	salt and pepper to taste

[*]For more information about the *Hobo Times,* write the National Hobo Association Inc., P.O. Box 706, Nisswa, MN 56468

First catch, by whatever method, five or six pigeons. Cut their breasts out (thus, no need for plucking), eviscerate the breast cavity, wash with water, and skewer the meat on a couple of green branches. Pigeon meat is slightly oily (like a duck), so when braised over an open fire, the flesh surface glazes and holds in the juices. Once the braising is done, place the browned breasts in enough water to cover and let them boil gently for about a half-hour. To this stock of pigeon broth, add a small amount of water along with quartered onions, unpeeled wedges of potatoes, and celery or carrots, if available. Next, add a shallow palm (about a tablespoon) of salt, pepper as needed, and continue to boil the whole shebang gently. Periodically add water, but not so much that the flavor is lost. After about an hour, the breast can be penetrated with a pocketknife point. Add two or three palms of cornstarch and stir. Flour will also work, but cornstarch doesn't lump. Bring the pot to a more vigorous boil for three to five minutes, stirring all the time. Voila! Creamed squab à la jungle—with a side order of salted corn on the cob, a meal par excellence!

Boxcar Breakfast

by Gypsy Moon

"Hit the Road" Egg Casserole

3 cups cooked ham or sausage	8 eggs
8 slices white bread	2 cups milk
1/2 lb. grated sharp cheddar	salt and pepper to taste

Layer twice in well-oiled Dutch oven: ham, bread (broken into pieces), and cheese. Beat eggs, milk, and seasonings. Pour wet mixture over layered ingredients in the Dutch oven. Cover with lid. Bake one hour.

Fast Track Cinnamon Biscuits

2 large cans refrigerator
  biscuits

melted margarine
cinnamon and sugar

Place biscuits close together in large (20 inch) skillet with Dutch oven lid. Brush with margarine and sprinkle generously with cinnamon and sugar. Bake for 15 to 20 minutes. Keep Dutch oven slightly farther from heat than usual and use fewer coals on lid to prevent scorching.

Apple Tramp Breakfast Pie

3 cups diced apples
1 cup sugar
1 cup flour

1 stick margarine, melted
1 cup brown sugar

Place apples in Dutch oven; dump sugar on top. Mix other ingredients, pour over apples, and bake until brown—about 45 minutes.

Walking Stick Potatoes

3 large potatoes, pared
5 slices crumbled cooked
  bacon

salt and pepper to taste
1 large onion, sliced
1/2 cup margarine, sliced

Mix all ingredients in large, doubled sheet of foil (allow some room for steam expansion). Seal well and bake in coals for 45 minutes to an hour. Flip bundle occasionally with walking stick.

Cajun Hotshot
by Hobo Troubadour Liberty Justice

Libby's Chili

1/2 lb. bacon
1 cup lard
2 tbs. white flour
2 jalapeño peppers
1 medium onion (chopped)
3 lb. boneless pork roast
1 tsp. Louisiana Cajun
   seasoning
1 tsp. lemon pepper
1 tsp. cayenne pepper

2 tbs. cumin
2 tbs. Louisiana Hot Sauce
1 quart tomatoes
6 corn tortillas
1 tbs. grated garlic
2 red chili peppers
2 cans red beans
2 cans ranch style pinto
   beans
1 large alligator

Using large cast iron skillet, fry bacon. Add enough lard to make about a cup. Heat until very hot. Sift flour into lard and brown. Grate jalapeño peppers and chop onion into lard and brown. Add pork (cut into pieces) and brown to seal in flavor. Put Cajun seasoning, lemon pepper, cayenne pepper, cumin, and Louisiana Hot Sauce into blender with tomatoes. Let blender run at high speed about 5 seconds. Crush tortillas until they look like cornmeal. Pour both mixtures and grated garlic, chopped chili peppers, and crushed tortillas into a large pot and cook about 2 hours. Add beans and let simmer on low heat for 30 to 45 minutes. Now give a sample to your alligator. If he doesn't start smoking from the ears, you can try it! Serve with fresh corn or flour tortillas or roll up in soft tortillas and eat like burritos. If eating in a hobo jungle, it is perfectly acceptable to let the juice run down your arms. Have a *large* glass of cold water nearby!

A Healthy Way to Start the Day

by Oats

Oats is one of many vegetarians in the hobo community.

A.M. Oats

1 banana
2 tsp. raisins
1 cup rolled oats
1 tbs. each of sunflower
    seeds, sesame seeds,
and wheat germ, if
    available
fruit juice and milk
honey

Slice 1/3 banana into bowl. Add raisins and 1 cup rolled oats. Mix in tablespoon of sunflower and sesame seeds and wheat germ. Pour in equal portions of fruit juice and milk. Top with honey. Do not cook!

All-American Iron-Rail Grillout

by Ink Man

Simply prop a grate from an old grill (be sure it's clean!) on a couple of rocks a few inches above the hot embers of the fire, and presto—you're ready for an instant hobo grillout!

Hallelujah, on a Bun! Simple and Easy

1 1/2 lb. ground beef
1/2 cup chopped onion
salt and pepper to taste
1 cup catsup
2 tsp. Worcestershire sauce

Combine beef, onion, and salt and pepper. Pat into several thick patties. Broil on the grill for about 10 minutes. Mix the two remaining ingredients and heat separately. Brush burgers with sauce. Each hobo can add extra sauce as desired with the meal.

The following baked apples and glazed ham can also be served with boiled eggs for breakfast:

Baked Apples

8 cored apples   cinnamon and sugar to taste
1 large strawberry soda   a sprinkle of raisins if desired

Place apples in a Dutch oven and pour the strawberry soda over them. Bake covered for 35 to 45 minutes. Sprinkle with cinnamon and sugar during the last 10 minutes of baking.

Glazed Ham

Use ham slices which are already fully cooked. Broil them over the fire for about 10 minutes so that ham does not dry out. Brush generously the last few minutes with sauce from baked apple recipe (above).

Ink Man Speaks Out about Steaks

For juicy steaks with a nice brown coating, grill for the first 2 or 3 minutes near the fire to seal in juices. For the best flavor, halve a clove of garlic and rub on steaks before grilling—then toss the remaining garlic in the fire under the steaks. Steaks can also be basted during cooking with a mix of melted butter and lemon.

Sweet and Simple
by Minneapolis Jewel

Minneapolis Jewel, twice elected by the hobos as their National Queen, is known for her kindness to the 'bos, her rail-jumping adventures, and her good cooking. In Britt's jungle these recipes have been tried, tested, and overwhelmingly, unanimously approved in taste tests—breakfast after breakfast after hobo breakfast!

Simple Hobo Bread

3 cups self-rising flour
3 tbs. sugar

1 12-ounce can of beer
(room temperature)

Mix all ingredients together and bake at 375° for 45 minutes in a greased 9 x 5 inch loaf pan. This can also be baked in a Dutch oven with lid over an open fire by putting a few (not too many) hot coals on the lid and under the pot.

Wild Plum Jam

8-10 cups wild plums
(easily found near tracks
in summer)

1 cup water
1 pkg. Sure-Jell
6 cups sugar

Gather, wash, halve, and pit plums (leave skins on). Put in large pot and add water. Cook 15 minutes to soften fruit. Add Sure-Jell and bring to full rolling boil, stirring constantly. Add sugar and continue boiling for 1 minute, still stirring. Remove from heat, skim off any foam, and ladle jam into mason jars with lids. Can be refrigerated for longer storage. This same recipe can be used by substituting other fruit such as apples or rhubarb.

A Gift from a Hobo Princess
by Little Princess Sarah Gilbert

Sarah lives in Britt, Iowa, home of the National Hobo Convention. Throughout the year, she keeps a steady vigil by walking daily to the jungle site and counting the days until her hobo friends return. In 1990, to show their appreciation, the hobos dubbed her a hobo princess. She was nine years old. She brings her special bread as a gift to the hobos during their August gathering, because she is ape over hobos.

Ape-over-Hobos Monkey Bread

4 pkgs. buttermilk biscuits	Topping:
1/2 tsp. cinnamon	1 cup sugar
3/4 cup brown sugar	1 tsp. cinnamon
	1 1/2 sticks of butter

Put sugar and cinnamon in a paper bag. Cut each biscuit in four pieces. Shake the pieces in bag mixture and drop them into a bundt pan. Bring topping ingredients to a boil and pour over biscuits. Bake at 350° for 40 minutes. Remove from pan as soon as bread is done.

A Road Meal Made Easy
by Ragman

Quick Fix Tummy Delight

Since hobos are a thrifty lot, monetary consideration plays a part in recipes. This is a good, cheap meal that has served me well on the road. I carry a package of Ramen noodles in my pack. They don't add much weight, they only cost about a quarter, and you simply add hot water to cook. If you want to dress the noodles up a bit, check the local grocery store's dumpster for veggies that have just been thrown out. Don't worry if they have a few specks; they can be cut away during cleaning. I especially like to cook mushrooms, cauliflower, broccoli, and onions in a gun boat (empty coffee can) of water and add them to the noodles. Sometimes gardeners and farmers are quite generous, too. To season, just add a fast-food packet or two of salt and pepper to taste. (Hobos always grab a few extra packets for their pack!) If available, it adds great flavor and nourishment to crack a couple of eggs into the mixture. (I always keep my eyes open for a nearby chicken pen!)

Occasionally on the road, I open the noodles and eat them raw. Nice and crunchy.

Jungle Basics

by Be-Gone Norm

Norm's 239 Bean Soup

(Because one more bean makes it too "forty"!)

1 lb. soup beans (northern or navy)	2 large onions, chopped
	4 carrots, chopped
1 1/2 lb. butt end portion of a ham	4 potatoes
	Dash of red hot pepper sauce
2 cups celery, diced	Sprinkle of black pepper

Soak beans in soda water (enough to cover) overnight. Cover ham with cold water and bring to boil until tender (skim off fat). Drain water from beans, rinse, and add fresh water (enough to cover). Cook until almost soft. Add cooked ham (and broth) and all other ingredients. Continue cooking until vegetables are soft.

Norm's Potato and Rivel Soup

5 potatoes, diced
1 onion, chopped
1 quart heated milk
salt and pepper to taste

7 slices bacon, chopped
1 cup plus 3 tbs. flour
1 beaten egg

Boil potatoes and onion in a little water until soft. Add heated milk and season with salt and pepper to taste. Fry bacon and brown 3 tbs. flour in a couple tbs. bacon grease. Slowly blend potato mixture in. Combine 1 cup flour, salt and pepper to taste, and beaten egg until mixture becomes crumbly. Rub through hands into hot soup. Continue cooking 10 minutes more.

Norm's Creek Bank Chowder

4 lb. catch-of-the-day fish,
    cleaned
8 slices bacon, diced
2 large onions, diced

5 potatoes
1 quart scalded milk
salt and pepper to taste

Boil fish, bone and flake. Fry bacon, remove from pan. Sauté onion in bacon fat. Cook potatoes in enough water to cover. Add bacon, onions, flaked fish, and scalded milk to potato/water mixture. Simmer together and serve with crackers.

Norm's Muskrat or Rabbit

muskrat or rabbit (dressed/
    soaked overnight in
    salt water)
2 onions, chopped

4 stalks celery, chopped
4 carrots, chopped
salt and pepper to taste
butter or margarine

Drain salt water off meat, wash in clean cold water. Cover with fresh water and put in kettle. Add onion, celery, carrots, salt and pepper and bring to boil over the open fire. Remove foam and simmer until meat is fork tender. Remove meat and drain. Pitch out liquid and vegetables since their purpose was to take wild flavor from meat. Pat meat dry, cut up, and brown in buttered skillet over a low fire. This is great served alongside boiled potatoes and sweet and sour cabbage.

Norm's Outdoor Chicken Rice or Barley Soup

whole chicken (can substitute turkey)	salt to taste
2 tbs. butter	pepper sauce to taste
1/2 cup celery, chopped	1 large onion, diced
1 cup carrots, diced	1/2 cup rice or barley

Cover carcass with water and simmer 2 hours, covered. Drain meat, remove meat from bone, cut in pieces, and set aside. In large saucepan, melt butter. Add celery, carrots, salt, pepper sauce, and onion. Sauté until tender. Add meat pieces and broth and rice (or barley). Bring to a boil. Reduce heat and simmer 30 minutes over low fire or until grain is fully cooked.

Flophouse Favorites
by Midwest John, hobo singer/songwriter

Ham and Beans

2 lb. navy beans	2 tsp. salt
2 large onions, chopped	2 tsp. garlic
6 large potatoes, chopped	1/4 cup brown sugar
4 large ham hocks	2 tsp. pepper
1 lb. bacon, fried	1/4 tsp. cumin
1/4 cup mustard	1/4 tsp. thyme
1 lb. carrots, chopped	1/4 tsp. basil

Clean beans. Soak in large pot for 30 minutes in 2 gallons of water. Add other ingredients. Cook until beans are done. Thicken with cornmeal; thin with water. Add more seasoning to taste.

Midwest John's Corn Bread

2 cups flour	1/4 cup bacon grease
2 cups cornmeal	1 1/2 cups milk
1/4 cup sugar	2 tbs. baking powder
1/4 cup brown sugar	1 cup water

3 eggs

Mix in bowl. Bake in well-greased, covered cast iron skillet or in conventional oven for 15 to 20 minutes or until browned.

Hot and Hearty, but Not in a Hurry
by Burma Shave, the Thumb Tramp

Burma Shave enjoys working in the kitchen each year at the National Hobo Convention. "I've learned much from Fry Pan Jack, the jungle's 1st cook," he says. "Anyone else is a 2nd cook, a pearl diver, or a kitchen dog (prep worker)." Jungle Jambalaya is a Burma Shave special.

All-Day-Long Jungle Jambalaya

5 lb. dried beans (northern whites are suitable)
3-4 whole chickens, cut up
salt and pepper
1 big spoonful cayenne
onion and garlic salt
paprika
1 lb. bacon, chopped into 1-inch pieces
4-5 big onions, chopped (set 1 aside to sprinkle in after all is done)
1 head celery, chopped
1-2 heads garlic, peeled and chopped fine
4-5 green bell peppers, seeded and chopped
3 lb. Polish kielbasa
1 1/2 lb. hot Italian sausage
1 1/2 lb. mild or sweet Italian sausage
1 big can V-8 juice
1 #10 can tomatoes, chopped
1 big handful thyme
3-4 bay leaves
1 small bottle Lee & Perrins
4-5 smoked ham hocks
3 lb. uncooked rice
1 large bunch scallions, chopped small
1 bunch parsley, chopped fine

Night before: Soak beans in twice enough water to cover. Rub the chicken with black pepper, cayenne, garlic salt, onion salt, and paprika. Cover and refrigerate overnight.

Next day: Fry bacon in stew pot until brown; set aside. Add onions and celery to bacon grease and cook over low fire until brown. Add garlic and green peppers; cook until soft. Remove vegetables (set aside), leaving grease (add cooking oil if needed). Add sausages and brown. Meanwhile, cut all sausages to 1/2 inch. When chicken is done, return the vegetables and sausage to pot; add V-8, tomatoes, thyme, bay leaves, Lee & Perrins, and bacon. Drain water off beans; add to pot with ham hocks. Add hot water or stock to cover ingredients. Bring to boil, then cook slowly until beans are done. Fish out chicken and ham and cut all meat off bones before returning it to pot. Add rice (and more water or stock if needed) and cover to cook another 1/2 hour. Toss in scallions, parsley, and reserved onions. Serves 50+.

Stirring Up Turtle Stew and Memories

Bo Britt Eddie's Turtle Stew

1 medium or large turtle (snapper preferred), de-shelled and skinned	1 cup chopped onions
	1 1/2 cups chunked celery
	2 cups chunked carrots
2 or 3 beef soup bones	1 cup sliced rutabaga
salt and pepper	2 cups chunked potatoes

Step #1: Cut meat from upper legs and neck (save for frying or roast). Use bones, lower legs, neck, and tail for stew. Simmer beef soup bones in about 3 quarts of water. Remove bones from broth when done and pick lean meat from bones (discard bones). Skim fat from broth if desired.

Step #2: Add turtle meat to broth and cook until meat can easily be removed from bones. Pick meat from bones (discard bones).

Step #3: Season broth with salt and pepper and add vegetables and cook until nearly done. Add the lean beef and turtle meat until veggies are completely done. Add more seasoning as desired.

Hints: For thicker stew, add a thin paste made of flour and cold water; for thinner consistency, add more water or broth. If your turtle is small, use all the meat for stew. Veggies can vary according to taste, but I prefer only root vegetables except for a few green beans.

Bo Britt Eddie's Turtle Stew on the Narrow Gauge
by Luther the Jet

The old Milwaukee Road had many strange and wondrous operations, but none more fantastical than the River Line, a twisting, curving 160-mile stretch of track along the west bank of the Mississippi River that connected the St. Paul main at La Crescent, Minnesota, with the Omaha and Kansas City mains at Sabula, Iowa. Unlike the high-speed Burlington, which occupied the Mississippi's east bank in these latitudes, the River Line was a meandering, circuitous route whose alignment took full account of every slough and backwater in the river. Between ancient steamboat landings and high limestone bluffs, the River Line plunged through forests in a country that even today is wild and scenic, revered for centuries by Native Americans and still held in awe by wanderers and dreamers of every stripe.

And the River Line had branches, two of them built as narrow gauge, and all running through country so difficult that they can still excite the imagination, even after they've been torn up for years. The branches followed long coulees—deep, tortuous valleys that wound their way up from the river bottoms to the high, corn-bearing plains. This countryside is heavily wooded, frequently shrouded in mist, and even in the full light of day often seems like a land that time forgot.

Headquarters of the River Line was at Marquette, Iowa. Here the old Iowa & Dakota Division came down off the plains, crossed the River Line at right angles, and went over the Mississippi on a long pontoon bridge, one of only two railroad pontoon bridges in the United States (the other was at Wabasha, Minnesota).

Marquette, shorn of most of its facilities, still serves as the junction between the River Line and the I&D, both of them now part of the CP Rail system. In addition to Marquette, each of the branches had its own separate terminal—at Reno, Waukon Junction, Turkey River, and Bellevue. Except for Bellevue, these places are ghost towns today, or nearly so, with only a few oldtimers left who can recall the depots, engine houses, water tanks, jungles, boarding houses, stores, hotels, bars, and bordellos that once made them thrive.

Keeper of the flame at Reno is hobo poet and historian Bo Britt Eddie Colsch, who was born in 1911. He was raised in the area and hoboed along the River Line and the Reno Branch from the time he was a teenager, beginning in 1937, until he was drafted into the Army in 1942. He and his wife Evelyn live in a solid old farmhouse, built in 1868 and purchased by Eddie's grandfather. Here he and Evelyn raised nine children.

Eddie asked me if I wanted to come take a look at the country he grew up in. I sure did.

There was an added inducement, as Eddie explained on the phone: "My son just caught a turtle, a big male snapper that crawled up out of the river into his backyard. I got it all cleaned and cut up and put away in the freezer. We'll have some turtle stew when you get here. We'll set up our stew pot on the west end of the wye at Reno, right by the slough where the hobos used to jungle up."

Who could resist an invitation like that?

When I arrived, Eddie had already cooked up the carrots and onions and put them in a separate pot. We peeled and sliced potatoes while the turtle meat simmered on the woodburning stove. When the meat was done, we let it cool off in a pan, then picked through it with knife and fork to cut up the chunks and remove any small pieces of bone. Turtle is supposed to contain seven different kinds of meat, which resemble chicken, veal, rabbit, and so forth.

When the preliminaries were complete, we packed everything into the trunk of Eddie's car and headed down the dirt road to Reno. After carrying everything down a hill, we set up our fire right on the grade of the old narrow-gauge wye. Soon it was late afternoon, and the stew was bubbling away. By suppertime about twenty people had gathered around the fire. We sang a few songs, swatted mosquitoes, listened to some tall tales, and polished off a case of beer and some of the best turtle stew ever made.

I trust the spirits of the old 'bos who jungled up here were with us, for it was definitely part of Eddie's plan that they should be summoned and included.

Glossary

Ballast—The gravel used for rail beds.
Bay Horse—Brand name of rubbing liniment for horses. Similar to bay rum.
Bindle—A bedroll.
Blind—Front end of a baggage car.
Bridge and plank gang—A railroad maintenance crew.
Bridger—A hobo who rode both steam-powered and diesel-powered trains.
Bull—A policeman.
Canned heat—Strained Sterno consumed for the alcohol content.
Catch the westbound—Die.
Cinder bull—A railroad policeman.
Consist—All the cars that make up a particular train.
Couplers—Fixtures at the ends of train cars used to connect one car to the other.
Courtesy call—A night's stay in the town jail without being arrested. An opportunity to get in out of the cold and to eat a meal.
Crummy—Caboose.
Dick—A detective.
Drag—A slow freight train.
Dumpster diving—Rummaging through dumpsters for food or other needed items.
Freddy—Flashing rear-end device on the train. It has taken the place of the caboose.
Gay cat—A person on the road who, when the going gets tough, can afford to purchase a ticket (Irwin 84).
Go in the hole—To pull onto a siding to allow another train of higher priority to pass by.
Gondola—A train car with low walls and no roof.
Gun boat—An empty can used for cooking. Usually a coffee can.
Harness bull—A policeman in uniform.

Helper—An extra engine added temporarily to a train to assist in pulling it up a steep grade.

High iron—The track in a railroad yard that serves as the main line or through line.

Hooverville—Shantytowns built of junk and cardboard by the poor. Named after Herbert Hoover, the 31st president of the United States of America (1929-1933).

Hotshot—A fast train.

Jackrollers—Thieves who often targeted a hobo who had just received his pay.

Jocker—A man who travels the road with an underage boy.

Jungle—An encampment where hobos stayed for brief periods before moving on. "To jungle up" is to stay in a jungle.

Jungle buzzard—Someone in a hobo jungle who tries to avoid sharing in the work and expense.

Knee-shaker—A handout on a plate at the back door of a house. Eaten on the back steps while balancing the plate on one's knees.

Knuckle—A movable joint in the coupler.

Live train—A consist of railcars with engines hooked to it. A train that could move at any time.

Local—A train that makes many stops and does much work in a short distance.

Lump—A handout which is packaged to be taken along on the road.

Mission stiff—A bum that spends much time in missions.

Mixed freight—A train consisting of a variety of cars.

"P" farms—Farms where prisoners worked.

Pearl diver—A dishwasher.

Punk—A young boy traveling on the road with an older man.

Rattler—A long train rattling along the tracks, resembling a rattlesnake.

Red cards—A membership card of the International Workers of the World (IWW).

Reefer—A refrigerated freight car.

Rods—The steel structural bars that were below the old boxcars. A very dangerous and difficult place for hobos to ride.

Rule of the match—An insulting gesture of handing a match to someone. It is the same as saying, "You are not welcome around this jungle fire. Go build your own someplace else."

Scoping the drag—Looking for a good ride on a freight train as it slows down.

Seam squirrels—Lice.

Sit-down—A meal given as a handout with the offer to eat it in comfort at the kitchen table.

Specks—Fruit with spots beginning to form. Farmers and groceries were often willing to give it to hobos.

Stack train—A train made up of topless, low-sided cars which carry large containers sometimes stacked two high.

Streamliners—Railriders that travel with light gear and on fast freights.

Walking dandruff—Lice.

Wobblies—A short name for the International Workers of the World (IWW).

Yard dick—A railroad detective.

Hoboes used their own system of marks, a code by which they left information and warnings to their fellow Knights of the Road. Here is a sampling of the many symbols left on fence posts, gates, railroad section shanties, bridges and water tanks.

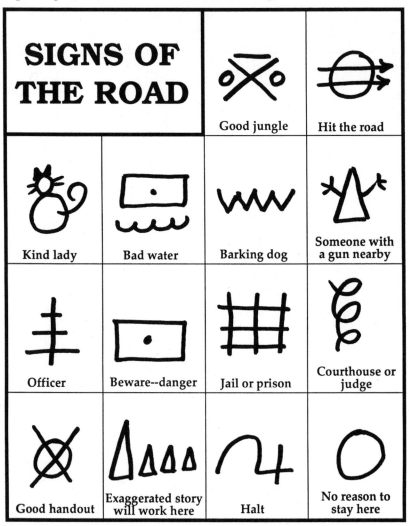

SIGNS OF THE ROAD

Good jungle	Hit the road	
Kind lady	Bad water	Barking dog	Someone with a gun nearby
Officer	Beware--danger	Jail or prison	Courthouse or judge
Good handout	Exaggerated story will work here	Halt	No reason to stay here

References

Allsop, Kenneth. *Hard Travellin': The Hobo and His History.* London, England: Hodder and Stoughton, 1967.

Anderson, Nels. *The Hobo: The Sociology of the Homeless Man.* Chicago: University of Chicago Press, 1961. 1st ed. 1923.

Bruns, Roger. *Knights of the Road.* New York: Methuen, 1980.

"For Hoboes." *Time,* 17 May 1937.

Garraty, John A. *The American Nation: A History of the United States.* New York: Harper and Row, 1966.

"Hobo Hegemony." *Literary Digest,* 10 April 1937.

Irwin, Godfrey. *American Tramp and Underworld Slang.* New York: Sears Publishing Company, 1930.

"Ladies of the Road." *Literary Digest,* 13 August 1932.

Milburn, George. *The Hobo's Hornbook: A Repertory for a Gutter Jongleur.* New York: Ives Washburn, 1930.

Reckless, Walter. "Why Women Became Hoboes." *American Mercury,* February 1934.

"Tramps." *The Nation,* 9 August 1933.

Jacqueline K. Schmidt, *a graduate of Indiana University, is the former Executive Director of the Indiana Transportation Museum. Her interest in railroads and hoboing, piqued by her father's stories of his life on the road, led her to begin a series of oral histories with oldtime hobos who lived on the road in her father's time. Soon she was leaving her cabin in southern Indiana for extended rail trips with her vagabond friends. The hobo community accepted her into its midst by honoring her with her road name, Gypsy Moon, and in 1990 elected her a National Queen of the Hobos.*